ADVANCE PRAISE FOR DEAL JUNKIE

"Who doesn't LOVE GILBERT HARRISON!
The ultimate dealmaker."
—**Tommy Hilfiger,** Fashion Icon

"Gilbert has been the cornerstone in keeping the
American cosmetic business on track."
—**Leonard Lauder,** Chairman Emeritus of
The Estée Lauder Companies Inc.

"Gilbert Harrison has always been the best source of
what's happening in our retail and fashion world."
—**Stuart Weitzman,** Shoe Designer and
Founder of Stuart Weitzman

DEAL JUNKIE

A HALF-CENTURY OF DEALS THAT BROUGHT
THE BIGGEST U.S. RETAIL AND APPAREL COMPANIES
TO ANSWER THE MOMENT AND PREPARE FOR THE FUTURE

GILBERT HARRISON

POST HILL
PRESS

A POST HILL PRESS BOOK
ISBN: 978-1-63758-132-2
ISBN (eBook): 978-1-63758-133-9

Deal Junkie:
A Half-Century of Deals that Brought the Biggest U.S. Retail and Apparel
Companies to Answer the Moment and Prepare for the Future
© 2022 by Gilbert Harrison
All Rights Reserved

This is a work of nonfiction. All people, locations, events, and situations are portrayed to the best of the author's memory.

Post Hill Press
New York • Nashville
posthillpress.com

Published in the United States of America
1 2 3 4 5 6 7 8 9 10

For my mother,
Trese Warner Harrison,
and my wife, Shelley.

TABLE OF CONTENTS

Gilbert at the start of his
career in the 1970s.

A Crisis of Passion and a Big Bounce Back: The Lehman Brothers Boom, Bust, and Rebirth Years

FOURTEEN YEARS AFTER STARTING MY investment banking firm, Financo, I sold it to Shearson Lehman/American Express. The year was 1985. An inauspicious sign at the start: my first day there was Steven Schwarzman's last. I said to Steven that morning, "Why are you leaving?" and he said to me, "Why are you coming?"

Well, it should have been a terrific opportunity, from my time as a mid-sized dealmaker working primarily in Philadelphia to joining on as a Managing Director of what was then one of the premier firms in the world. I won't lie: I loved my office view. Lehman had just moved their offices from 55 Water Street to the World Financial Center, and I had a corner office looking out at the Statue of Liberty. My wife Shelley and I had just bought a pied-à-terre on 72nd and Madison, and we were going back and forth between our home in Philadelphia and the new apartment. New York was but a short ride on the Amtrak, but I had the luxury of a driver so going back and forth during the week-days and weekends between the Big Apple and the City of Brotherly

Love was not a problem. My driver was a fantastic person, very good to me over the years, and was also most helpful in bringing me from my Upper East Side apartment to my downtown office and then back uptown for client meetings, the headaches of gridlock notwithstanding. New York was not at its peak beauty back then. The city was coming through hard times. The whole country was. Reagan was about to become the next big thing in the White House. The excess that we generally associate with the 1980s, and in particular Wall Street, was nigh. And me? I was looking out each day at Lady Liberty, so moved up in the world. Being bought by Lehman—this was the epitome of success. Best of all, I would be able to start doing the very biggest mergers and acquisitions in the country. In fact, I was not unfamiliar with working on such kinds of deals. Financo had recently completed two major acquisitions. The first of these was the purchase of Hasbro for Milton Bradley for about five hundred million dollars. Perhaps you think a company like Milton Bradley is all Barrel of Monkeys, Battleship, Trouble, and Operation. Well, it *is* those things. But while at the heights of its success and owning such games as Monopoly, buying Hasbro allowed it to grow significantly.

The second deal was the sale of Brooks Fashion Stores to AEA Investors and Dylex Corporation, which at the time was one of Canada's largest retailers. This was another deal with a huge fee. Both deals were among the ten largest deals of their yearly quarters.

So, my business was going strong. The mergers and acquisition market had gotten extremely hot. But this doesn't explain why Lehman had come knocking on my door. That story begins in 1983 when Michael Milken made his own approach to buy Financo. I had known Michael since he'd made his start in Philadelphia after getting his MBA at Wharton. One of my best friends was at Drexel Burnham where Michael was a rising star and, through him, we got to know each other very well. After some time, Michael became interested in retail and the cash flow coming from these companies, and he asked me if I would consider joining Drexel Burnham, either bringing

Financo along with me, or, just coming along myself. It was intriguing but I was concerned about the lifestyle in LA. Their office would start its business day around five o'clock in the morning, and they would work until after the sun had set. Because of these demands, many of his people I knew were either having heart attacks, getting divorced, or both. I credit my wife Shelley for refusing to let me and our family go down that path. But I was still interested enough in a potential partnership with Drexel to speak with one of my closest friends on Wall Street, Peter Solomon, who was then the Vice Chairman of the Investment Banking Group at Shearson, Lehman, Hutton American Express. His advice to me was that, instead of going over to Drexel, I should join Shearson, Lehman to head their Merchandising Group, which included apparel, retail, footwear, and other consumer groups.

And so I did.

Despite all of the financial gain that had come with the sale of Financo, I had not sold to Lehman for the money, nor for the prestige or the tickets to Wimbledon and the flights on the Concorde—although I must say, I did love those Concorde flights *very* much—but because a larger firm could give me more resources and bring me into the senior leagues to do the absolute biggest deals around. As previously noted, while I had orchestrated five-hundred-million-dollar deals, the bulk of our business was still middle market transactions, which, at the time, ranged in value from thirty million to a hundred million dollars. But I wanted the ability to play in the big leagues and do something meaningful at the highest level. The thing is, I love deals. I love everything about them: the game, the interactions with people, the chase, the kill. I always have, going all the way back to those earliest deals hashed out in the living room between myself, my brother, my mother, and father during my childhood in 1950s New Haven, Connecticut. But let's not talk about those days quite yet. First, let me tell you how Lehman, in just a few short years, nearly snuffed out that love and drove me to do as Steve Schwarzman had done the day I had arrived at the company: head for the door.

Now maybe you recall that Lehman Brothers went bust in September of 2008. (I don't think anyone doesn't remember.) Well, all the signs of a collapse were already in place when I arrived in the mid-1980s. You had the politics of the old Lehman Brothers, and you had the bureaucracy that came from their parent company, Shearson/American Express. The in-fighting, envy, and divisions within the company's structure made it so that you were working not as a team but against the people in your own office. Very few of the bankers shared information. There was very little camaraderie. The bankers, for instance, were all very hesitant about sharing deals, concerned that doing so would affect their bonuses—and so they wanted to work on everything themselves and bar anyone else from receiving what should have been their business. That made for a very difficult environment. My friend, Daniel Good, who had also come to Lehman from another firm, was head of merchant banking at the time, and he explains it like this:

> "Most new top-level recruits didn't see or appreciate these conflicts as they weren't apparent from the outside. But what should have been a comfortable and effective joint effort became a war zone over fee sharing and credit for transactions. As a result, internal tumult ensued, and top management changed several times before stability was achieved."

I hadn't seen any of it from the outside, no, but now that I was on the inside at Lehman it was all disappointingly apparent. And then something happened that really took the bloom off the rose.

You see, before I had come to Lehman, back when they were courting me, I had been told by them that Macy's was their longest, most important retail client. Naturally, I had long admired Macy's and greatly looked forward to working with them. But then, a month or so after my arrival, I learned that Macy's had picked Goldman Sachs as their advisor in their bid to go private. Why? The only reason that anyone could conclude was because they believed Lehman had become a "second rate" firm. Have you ever seen Hitchcock's *Vertigo?* All of a sudden, that was me, with the office—and the Statue of Liberty with it—all starting to spin around and around and around. You wanted answers as to how this had happened, but you couldn't get any from anyone. It wasn't the kind of thing people discussed. And for the company, of course, it was treated as easy-come, easy-go. But no, this was Macy's. And I had joined Lehman so I could work with just these sorts of juggernauts. It was painful, disillusioning, and it had me looking around the office seriously doubting that this was the Lehman Brothers we all knew and revered.

While it took time, in just four years, over half of Lehman's investment banking operating committee of fifteen people had quit the company. One, two, three, four—*nine!* Nine of our fifteen committee members. And they were some of the best investment bankers on Wall Street. If you've ever been in a work environment where, one after another, the people you work with start to leave the company, you know that it's very tough on morale, and it makes it difficult to do your job. You don't know who's going to be there next week or next month, and you're wondering all the while whether you, too, shouldn't leave. Although my compensation was substantial, more than ever, I hated going to work each day. And the fact was, I couldn't shake the Macy's fiasco. Its message was too strong, too clear: "This company isn't what you thought it was when you signed up. You've got to get out. You've got to get the freedom to do what you do back. This isn't the place to grow. Who have you even become in this environment?"

I wasn't sure that I could even answer that question. With Financo independent in Philadelphia, I had been clear about myself and my job and how to go about it. I had known who I was and everyone around me had too. Now that feeling was gone. In fact, in Philadelphia, I was the "big fish" in a little pond. In New York and at Lehman, I was just another *schlepper.* But what was I going to do? Leaving Lehman wouldn't be easy, largely because I had signed a five year non-compete with them. Five years. There was no chance I would survive out there on my own for so long without doing the business I loved to do. I had no intention of subjecting myself or my family to that kind of uncertainty. But then, desperation isn't the worst sauce. It gets a guy thinking hard, and it makes him scrappy. And it made me see an opportunity.

At the time, I was working on three major deals. One was with Don Fisher, the founder and CEO of the Gap, exploring whether the company wanted to go private. The second was with Melville Corporation (which would become CVS in 1996) who was my biggest client at the time. We were working on two or three acquisitions for them. And the third was with Boston Stores, which was owned by the Swiss company Maus Frères, which was in the middle of acquiring Carson Pirie Scott Department Stores based in Chicago. They'd been my clients even before I went to Lehman. So, I went to Lehman, and I made them an offer that they could have refused but didn't: I would leave the company but continue to work on these three deals until they were seen through to an end. We agreed to a fee splitting in case any of them should work out. And that was that—they let me walk. The non-compete was put to bed. And, get this, I even got my company name back. Yep, that's right: Financo was returned to its founder, me. How I had missed it. How grateful I was to be able to fly that flag again. It's true, you don't know what you've got until it's gone. Or else you've got to set your love free, and if it comes back to you, then you know it's real. Either way, I was back in the saddle again—my own—ready to return to the fun of doing deals. I was reinvigorated. My love of the deal, a love that began early in life, all came rushing back to me, my blood warm, my eyes wide open.

Have you ever heard that story about the smart young boy who grows up to be president of the United States? Can you believe his mother, Bessie, was always disappointed that he wasn't a lawyer or a doctor? Thanksgiving comes and he calls his mother up in Fort Lauderdale, and he says, "Ma, I want you to come to the White House for Thanksgiving." The mother is reluctant to accept her son's invitation, but he tells her that he's going to send a limo and Air Force One to pick her up and *everything*. Finally, she says yes. Thanksgiving morning, she's leaving the lobby of her building to get into the car to go to the airport, and Bessie's friends say to her, "Where are you going?" And Bessie says, "You know my son the doctor and my other son the lawyer? I'm going to visit their brother."

Well, let's just say that this story applies to me and my parents too. Lawyer, doctor—these were the options my mother and father offered me at the time of my birth. Of course, you can't always please your mom and dad—and even though I went to law school, I always knew I liked business. Indeed, I showed an early instinct and passion for it.

I grew up four blocks from the Yale Bowl in New Haven, and my first job was selling programs before games. "Get your program here! Program! Program!" That was me, a young boy in the freezing cold on a late-autumn Northeastern day with rosy cheeks and big brown eyes, holding up my product and waving it in the air to get anyone to bite. Although I'd have a hoarse throat at the end of a day's work and need a cup of warm hot chocolate, it was an enjoyable job. Best of all, I got into the games for free and was able to see the action. And, wouldn't you know it, I learned that I liked a job that comped my tickets to sporting events.

"Each season Yale played either Princeton or Harvard at the Yale Bowl," says my dear brother, Roger. "The programs for those games were large and heavy and sold for one dollar as opposed to $.50 for the normal smaller programs for other Yale football games played in New Haven. The $1.00 programs were bulky, very big and heavy but very profitable as the commission on each program was around $.40 each. That presented a large opportunity to make money, perhaps $150, at that time a great amount for one afternoon of work."

It was a solid start in business. But then the next year a friend came to me with a new angle on generating income. Selling programs was great fun, sure, but how about we go into the big-time? Yes, the big-time. I was intrigued. Well, this friend lived just across the street from the Yale Bowl, and he had worked it out with his parents that we could park cars in front of his house at ten dollars a car. *Ten dollars a car*? Now this was a lot of money for a kid. And what percent did his parents want? 5 percent? 10 percent? They wanted nothing? Nothing at all? Just that their son and his friend could have a job and show some ingenuity? So, yes, I took the promotion, and suddenly I was making a lot of money. Walking around New Haven in those days, it was great to have money in my pocket. I realized then that I liked being able to buy most anything I wanted *when* I wanted, and I hoped (knowing that everything had its limits) that when I grew up, I wouldn't have it any other way.

But what did I even want? I was a teenager living in my parents' home, safe and well-cared for. My father had a chain of restaurants, bakeries, and candy stores in New Haven and around Connecticut called the House of Hasselbach, a block from the Yale University campus. You know that Norman Rockwell painting of the boy at the soda fountain? Okay, well, life inside the restaurant wasn't quite that serene, but you get the idea. It was what they like to call "simpler times." We knew a lot of people in New Haven, and everybody knew us. Children and their mothers and fathers would come in for ice cream and apple pie. You could have a cheeseburger for seventy cents, a BLT for fifty, a milkshake for thirty. Of course, nothing was new, and that was a beautiful thing, just as we liked it. What should be new? What should change? This life was working well for everyone, it seemed. I worked behind the counter at the House of Hasselbach during school vacations, helping out with the business. My father was a wonderful and kind man, very generous, well-liked. But he was also the first person to turn me down on a deal and teach me just how hard it can be to see a potentially good deal sour. My father had the most wonderful homemade pastries and cakes coming out of his bakeries—believe me, I ate my fair share, and they were outstanding, and I was called "pleasantly plump" as a result. People throughout New Haven and graduates of Yale all knew the quality of the product. Was he famous for it? Locally, yes, I would say he was exactly that. It occurred to me, however, that we could package and freeze his baked goods and begin selling them throughout the Northeast and maybe even to points south and west. Well, why not? We had this great big freezer where we used to make and store ice cream that had a lot of extra room inside it. We would only need to sell them in the store, package up the product in a spiffy box, and ship them off. I could already see my father's cakes and pastries in every supermarket in the country, on every table, in every mouth. But my father, blessed man, he looked at me and my mother, who *was* in support of my vision, and said, "I do not believe in frozen baked goods. If it's not fresh, it's no good."

"Dad, I don't know. I think you ought to rethink this. I think this could mean big business."

But he didn't see it, and neither my mother nor I could *make* him see it. Though my father took pride in watching my career grow and prosper, I believe that this early professional dispute between us explains why, to this very day, I still feel a certain amount of regret when offered a Sara Lee poundcake.

My father was born and grew up in New Haven to parents who had emigrated from Russia. The family name is Hershasser, but when my father's father came through Ellis Island in 1888, the customs agent gave him the name Harrison since it started with an H and Benjamin Harrison was president. My grandfather was a grocer, who made ends meet and provided a humble origin for my own father, his brother, and my grandmother in a place built on the shoulders of immigrants. On the other hand, my mother, Trese Warner, was born and lived in New York City, and led a very privileged life growing up in a grand apartment on 96th Street with a butler and chauffeur. I was told that Cole Porter used to play at their dinner parties. Perhaps this is why my love of the good life feels almost to have been written into my DNA. My mother's family had emigrated from Germany around 1860 and might have been considered part of the "Our Crowd" old line of Jewish families with names like Sobel, Isaacs, Wolff, among others, and many with the first name of Gilbert. Her husband, my grandfather, was born in Romania and was a true entrepreneur—a millionaire two or three times over—who lost his fortune again and again. Initially, for instance, he was the largest importer of crystal glass into the US. Not bad—except that one day a machine was developed to press crystal, and my grandfather's millions of dollars' worth of inventory was suddenly worth less than nothing. Then the Depression came and, like most everyone, the family was hit hard. Also, at the same time, my mother's brother, Gilbert Warner, died of appendicitis at just sixteen before the advent of penicillin. (I was named after him and other ancestors.) Though my mother had had her eyes set on Wellesley College, her application already in the mail, my grandparents insisted that she stay close to home and her grieving family. She was still able to enroll at Barnard College and finish her studies and get her diploma. She got a job as a secretary to one of the directors at Pepsi Cola. She was very smart, industrious. Her boss used to have her put through his orders on Pepsi stock, and whenever she made the calls, she would buy one or two shares for herself. Five dollars here, ten dollars there. When she died at ninety-seven, she was sitting on more than $3 million in Pepsi stock. No one had any knowledge of her shrewd fiscal smarts. She had just been quietly putting a little away at a time. I did a cost analysis, providing for inflation, and calculated that she had spent fifty-eight cents on average for those stocks which sold at sixty-eight dollars each at the time of her death. So, there was a real savvy to my mother that worked hand in hand with a conservative nature brought on by her father's financial losses and their effect.

I did not want to go to Yale where I would be labeled a "townie," so I looked outside New Haven for school and was happy to be accepted at the Wharton School of the University of Pennsylvania, which was then—and still remains—the best undergraduate school of its kind. I majored in accounting. After graduating in 1962, I went to the School of Law at the University of Pennsylvania where I had one of the great lessons of my young adult life. My father was going through some difficult times financially. He had invested money into a failed real estate deal, and had also sold the restaurants. The family was struggling. For my mother, no question, fears of her own childhood and her father's financial ups and downs were weighing on her heavily. My parents had paid for my college, and the tuition for law school was up next. Necessarily, I had to start doing my share of work to, at the very least, relieve them of the financial burden of my living expenses. I was working at a travel agency in Philadelphia, and I began selling charter flights to Europe when affinity groups were just starting up. Using every connection I had with friends in schools around the Northeast, I drummed up interest in these trips to Europe. I spent a lot of time every day on the phone, reaching out to everyone I knew. "Buy a flight to Europe!" "Have you been to Europe? It's heaven on Earth!" "An American in Paris; that could be *you!*" I sold six hundred seats that first year, resulting in approximately $10,000 in income—an outlandish sum when you consider that three years later, in my first year of practicing law, my salary was $7,200. Now I know what you're wondering: Law school is highly demanding, isn't it? That's what they say. But if I was making all of this money in the travel industry, how much time did I spend studying? When did I learn the law and, most importantly, the ability to think, which is essential in both law and life? The truth was, I was not doing much of the above—and at the end of the school year, I was called in by the dean of the law school who informed me that I was flunking out and that he knew all about my business activities. He said I had a choice: I could stop working in the travel business and get down to my studies, or I could leave the school. This was a difficult decision, and not only because I was making more money than I could have ever dreamed. My family was not out of the woods yet as far as their own financial troubles were concerned. On the other hand, maybe it was time to tighten my own belt and scale back my entrepreneurial ambitions for the long game ahead. I had a whole life before me, and having a law degree was going to make that life (especially as it pertained to my hopes in a career of business), that much more successful. To have to pull back on a pursuit that was working out better than I could have ever hoped to better prepare for the marathon to come wasn't easy. It took that dean at the law school to bring it to my attention. I was just a young man. I needed that kind of guidance, the intellect of an experienced person to help show me that one step back can often mean two steps forward. I therefore made the decision to end my foray in the travel industry and continue on with my law studies, and when I graduated, I was in the top 10 percent of my class.

In 1965, I graduated law school and joined Mermelstein, Burns, and Lesser, a Park Avenue law firm in New York. My law work required long hours. I loved the people part of the law more than the legal side, but I dove in and worked primarily on mergers and acquisitions as well as other corporate work. I remember when the owner of the footwear retailer we represented known as Shoe Town Stores decided to be sold. Shoe Town had forty-two stores, and my task was to update forty-two different "minute books," as in those days each store was a separate corporation—a process done to save on taxes. I also had to work with the landlords to assign the leases to the new buyer, and this was all very time consuming. However, a week before the closing, the owner of Shoe Town made a new call. That was: "Forget it. We are not selling." So, my next job was to reverse everything I had done with respect to the minute books and leases. What a headache. But, it's important to remember where your professional life began. (As you will read later in this book, Lionel Levy, the owner of Shoe Town, would become a great client for whom we would sell Shoe Town three times.)

Skipping ahead, in 1971, while practicing law in Philadelphia at Blank Rome, the lawyer in the office next to me was Stephen Klein.

He and I became very close friends. In discussing our futures, we recognized that we both loved the clients we met day in, day out and enjoyed the negotiations of any deal, but that love did not extend to the legal work involved.

"I don't think either one of us was enamored with the law practice," says Stephen Klein. "But one thing that was good about that profession was that you could go down the hall and see a guy who was ten or twenty years older than you and decide whether that was the life that you wanted."

Well, we were each earning $25,000 a year and were six months away from becoming partners, at which point we would make $60,000—a large amount for the time. (However, one should note that the business brokers that we were dealing with at that time were making over $100,000 a year and were hardly what you would call professional. It's hard to look over your shoulder at brokers, in this case, who aren't as smart as you but are making three to four times your salary.) So, Steve and I began to consider leaving the firm. We initially explored partnering up with two well-known businessmen to buy one of the independent banks in Philadelphia and to use it as a basis to do deals. But that didn't work out, and instead we decided to strike out on our own and set up an investment banking firm. We went to see our boss, Samuel Blank, to resign. We had great admiration and respect for Sam Blank. He had treated us extraordinarily well, and we were both uneasy about informing him that our time at the firm was about to draw to a close. We weren't conflicted though. We knew it was time to move on—to move up, have new experiences, expose ourselves to greater challenges and create the possibility of reaping larger rewards. That's what we told Mr. Blank while standing shoulder to shoulder in his office—a couple of young lawyers trying to tell someone we respected and looked up to that we were leaving home. Mr. Blank said that a recession was imminent, and since we both had little children, we shouldn't put our futures at risk. His point struck a nerve in us. What kind of danger were we putting our families in? My daughter, Robin, was three, and my son, Ed, was six. What if our new venture failed? How would we provide for our growing families then? Steve and I went back to our offices, prepared to stay at the firm. But every night after, when I went to bed, I knew deep down that I was not on the path for which I was destined. Life had other things in store for me. I had to jump out into the unknown. The fear is very real. You feel it in your bones. What you don't know can and will hurt you. But without risk, what chance is there of a great reward? We all know the answer. Oftentimes it's looking you right in the eye. Well, Steve and I went back to Sam Blank a month later and said we were convinced that the right next step for us was to start our own investment banking firm. Sam Blank said to go with his blessings. But get this: Blank, *mensch* that he was, told us if things didn't work out, we could come back to work at the firm anytime, and our offices would be waiting for us. This was one of the nicest gestures ever made to me by another person in my professional life.

"He took the time and treated us in a very fatherly way," says Klein, "and I think it probably made an indelible impression on both me and Gilbert over our lifetimes as to how to treat people. Mr. Blank didn't have to do that. He just went out of his way and treated us with great respect and kindness."

And then there we were, two guys about to strike out on our own. We opened our offices in the IVB (Industrial Valley Bank) Building at 1700 Market Street in Philadelphia and began our firm.

"We had one secretary between us, and we'd fight over her—'I need her,' 'No, I need her,' 'But this is really important'—yes, that sort of thing," says Klein.

Luck was on our side. We got a referral to sell Ballaster Optical Company, a company based in Wilkes-Barre, Pennsylvania, which we sold to Itek in Boston and made our first fee: $180,000. Something you'll hear me say often throughout this book is that "that may not sound like a lot in today's dollars, but it was a bundle for the time." In

1971, $180,000 was equal to about $2 million or more in today's dollars. So yes, we were off and running.

Shortly after the Ballaster deal, I visited Bill Forman, the CEO of Devon Apparel. We'd taken the company public while at Blank Rome. Bill and his brother-in-law controlled the company, and we had become good friends. He knew that I had started an investment banking firm, and he wanted to help give me a start. Even though Bache was his banker, Devon Apparel decided to sell the company and offered us the right to represent them in the sale. We took our retainer—our first. One always remembers his first and second deals, and one also remembers his first retainer. You are forcing the company to show a commitment in you, to say that they are serious and not just on some hunting expedition to find the value of their company. Interestingly, at the beginning of our business careers, it was more difficult for me and Steve to get a $500–$1,000 retainer than it was for us to get a $100,000 retainer some ten years later. But such is the experience of starting out in the business world, being an unknown looking to prove your worth. With Devon Apparel, we prepared a selling memorandum, which was relatively easy because it had been less than two years since they'd gone public. We had the Prospectus, the Annual Report, and the SEC filings, so putting together a selling memorandum was an easier task than starting from scratch, especially having written prospectus and other materials while practicing law. We went to market, and from an article in the paper, we identified that Interco, the St. Louis-based shoe company known as the International Shoe Company (which also owned Florsheim) wanted to diversify their portfolio. I called the company and flew out to meet the chairman, Dude Chambers. Dude had started as a salesman and rose to become chairman, building the company up from a value of less than a $100 million to over a billion dollars. With a name like Dude Chambers, you can anticipate that there's not going to be a lot of bullshitting. There wasn't. Dude greeted me warmly but looked down at the Gucci shoes I was wearing on my size nine feet and said to me something I remember to this day:

"Son, if you come here to sell me a Lucky Strike, do not smoke a Camel."

I turned red. I wondered if the deal was off the table, kaput. But Dude then graciously gave me a Florsheim catalogue and had me pick out two pairs of Florsheim Shoes, which he gifted to me. I figured that if he was giving me two free pairs of shoes, it was very likely we were still in business. And we were. The deal went through, and Devon Apparel was acquired by Interco (and a solid relationship was built, as we sold them three other companies and advised them on many other matters). You better believe that whenever I went back to St. Louis or met with any of the Interco people in the years to come, I never failed to wear Florsheim shoes. To this day, when we are pitching a client and they are in the apparel or footwear industry, I try to wear one of their products and ask the associates attending with me to do the same—especially if the company is in women's apparel. Certainly, I cannot wear a dress. But all joking aside, we lost one deal with a shoe company because my banker wore a pair of shoes from a competitor brand. That was a tough lesson I will never forget.

Now I could keep going about those first ten or so years after we began Financo, listing all the deals that did and did not happen. For me, it would be nothing but a pleasure. However, that would cloud the real purpose of giving you my thoughts on my first years as an investment banker specializing in retail and apparel. The real purpose, the one that came back to me like a great bolt of lightning when I reacquired Financo from Lehman Brothers at the turn of the 1990s, is to call upon that energy and enthusiasm that propelled Steven and I like a couple of young thoroughbreds flying out of the gates and around the bends in the 1970s and early '80s. We had so much enthusiasm. We searched for opportunities with a hunger to be successful and the desire to bring great deals across the finish line. We were learning so much. We were meeting some of the greatest entrepreneurs in the country, people who had turned five-and-dimes into multi-million-dollar retail and apparel chains, little ma-and-pa hardware stores, shoe stores, and haberdasheries, that had grown into some of the most well-known national retail and apparel companies around. Even on the hardest days, when deals on which we'd worked ourselves to the bone fell through, we were propelled by a drive born of the love of what I do.

"Gilbert *really* loved what he was doing," says Klein. "He loved it. He just loved every part of it. He was excited. He was animated. He'd go to Timbuktu to meet a client. If the guy wanted to talk to Gilbert, away he'd go. He always had a big smile and a lot of energy, and he would do whatever it took to sign a client, to get a deal done. His love was at the core of what made him so successful, even at a young age."

But when Financo was sold to Lehman Brothers, I let the source of everything that keeps me moving forward in good and bad times take a severe hit. What I understood quite clearly after I got Financo back was to protect that source as you would your own life. For once you know the foundation of what keeps you hungry, excited to wake up each and every day and tackle the next opportunity, do not ever let it go. That's the only way to survive for over a half-century in this or any field where survival is not assured. Now, sit back and relax. Or, lean forward and pay close attention. We're going on a ride.

Gilbert with his partner Stephen Klein in their Financo offices
before the iconic Jasper Johns Corpse and Mirror artwork.

CHAPTER 1

Two Goliaths Walk into a Bar: Bringing Some of the Largest Egos to Ever Walk the Planet to the Bargaining Table

SHELLEY KAREN DANIEN IS MY wife of fifty-five years, best friend, and the mother of my three children. We were married on December 18th, 1965, in a beautiful ceremony at the Bellevue Stratford, which at the time was the very best hotel in Philadelphia. For our honeymoon, we went for a lovely stay in Bermuda. After returning, we settled into a one-bedroom apartment on Third Avenue in a newly constructed building which even had a balcony, and she and I became true lovers of New York City. New York was not yet in technicolor, though it soon would be. It was still that majestic place of long shadows, billowing cigar smoke of men in suits, cafes, Bobby Short and Ella Fitzgerald—"We'll have Manhattan/the Bronx and Staten Island too/It's lovely going through the zoo/It's very fancy on old Delancey Street, you know"—but also one where downtown in Greenwich Village the counter culture was already soaring. That is, all at once, it was a city straddling both the past and the future. As a young lawyer, it was long days and hard work, but Shelley brought a sense of ease and joy to my life. I often had to go downtown to file papers in court. (If you've ever watched an episode of *Law and Order*, you know just the buildings I'm talking about.) Anyhow, I detested the subway, especially in the summer as the heat was oppressive on the subway cars and, in those days, there was little to no air conditioning. If not for Shelley picking me up in our car and driving me to court from the law firm offices on Park Avenue, I would have sweat through my newly pressed shirts in seconds and shown up before the clerks or the judge looking like I was guilty of a crime I hadn't committed. But after my hours at court, as a reward to us both, I would take Shelley on a lunch date, just the two of us—a couple of kids in love enjoying a meal between the hustle and bustle. We also got invited to all the greatest parties. Why yes, because I happened to share a name with the owner and editor of the *New Republic* in those years—he was Gilbert A. Harrison; I am Gilbert W. Harrison—and we were constantly receiving his invitations to extravagant affairs. Usually, we'd turn them down, knowing that they were not for us. But, on occasion, I would put on a suit, Shelley a dress, and off we'd go into the glitzy New York night, no one knowing who we were.

On December 7th, 1966, Pearl Harbor Day, about one year after marrying and arriving in New York, Shelley gave birth to our son Edward Danien Harrison at Mount Sinai Hospital on the Upper East Side. Our family had now grown from two to three, and we were overjoyed. But then, as some of you may or may not know, living in a one-bedroom apartment in New York City with a baby is tight and hard on your spirits. Ed's crib was in the living room, and we had to move it if we had company. Well, this was hardly the dream. We were forging our lives, yes, pushing through those difficult, slim, early days, with each of us trying to figure out who we were and what we wanted and where we hoped to be in the years to come. We knew this wasn't it, that we weren't there yet, but we also understood that we had the foundation of a strong family, and this was a most important first step on our journey.

Shelley's father, Ed Danien, had gone to law school, worked for RCA and then struck out on his own at the start of WWII with Precision Plastics, making parts for the military and eventually, after the war, an assortment of toys and consumer products with injection moldings. I never was able to meet Ed (after whom my son is named). Tragically, at the age of forty-nine, he was killed on a Pan American flight coming back from a golfing trip in Puerto Rico. That was in December of 1963, two weeks after the assassination of President Kennedy. Shelley's mother, Florence Bass Danien, was a stunning, elegant woman whom I would grow to admire. She survived her husband's death with great strength and grace, as did Shelley and her brother, Marshall. In the time before his passing, however, Ed had been in the process of considering whether or not to go public with Precision Plastics. Now that he was no longer there to run things, my mother-in-law was left to consider such matters and to continue on at the helm of the family business. By 1967, she was doing a fine job in the position, but she asked Shelley and I if we would move down to Philadelphia and join the company. She needed us. And so, we went to her aid.

As a result of our decision, I resigned from Memelstein, and we packed our bags and moved to a wonderful garden apartment in the suburbs of Philadelphia. It was great to be back in the city where I had gone for both my undergraduate and law school education. Our son now had a bedroom of his own. Shelley was happy to be close to her family. She could now see them, as well as old friends, without having to travel. But despite these many positives, there was one problem, and it was a big one: Precision Plastics was not the job for me. Fact was, the practice of law let me work on a variety of transactions at the same time, and this new position was all about showing up and doing the same thing every single day. Do you like variety? Yeah, me too. It is, as they say, the spice of life. I like to put on different hats, go down different roads, come away with new information and experiences from one day to the next. But of course, we had only just arrived in town, and I had to dig in and give this new job my very best. Furthermore, this was my wife's family's business, and I felt a responsibility to do well and find the pleasure in it. Unfortunately, there were other overwhelming issues. My wife's cousin, who had been at Precision Plastics for years, didn't quite open his arms to the new guy in town with the fancy law degree and the firm backing of his aunt, my mother-in-law. Politics, power, control, they're always rearing their ugly heads, making already difficult jobs that much more difficult. I had some ideas about how to grow the company. I felt that the plastics vehicle could be expanded significantly as the world of mergers and acquisitions were in place and being touted as growth platforms in the late-1960s. I believed that there were opportunities to build a much larger company which we could then take public. "Just one word… plastics…There is a great future in plastics." Right? Even the biggest film of its time, *The Graduate*, knew the plastics industry had a "great future" ahead. But Shelley's cousin wouldn't hear it. He felt threatened and made things difficult for my mother-in-law, who depended on the income being generated by the company and didn't want to take any risks to jeopardize that. What could I do? What options did I have? I had left my job in New York, picked up the family, and come to Philadelphia. Now what?

Sam Blank, who I've already discussed, was the father of a law school friend and the senior partner of Blank Rome, a major firm in downtown Philadelphia. In pursuit of my next opportunity, I went to have a meeting with him and other partners from the firm. As fortune would have it, Sam asked me to join his law firm as an associate. I didn't walk but sprinted headlong towards this great new opportunity. Shelley supported the decision too. Though, because this was her family's business, my leaving was a sensitive issue for her and for all of us. She and I had many long conversations about it, and together we decided it was the right thing for me and our family, which now included a new baby girl, Robin.

Now, why do I tell you all of this about my personal history? Of course, before you take anyone's business advice or hear about where they've been in business, it's good to get to know them a bit. You want to know who they are, how they live, because it can only help you see the larger picture. And, for you to know the larger picture as it pertains to me, it is absolutely critical that you know about the central figure in my life—my wife, Shelley. Shelley's presence has been essential to some of the major decisions I've made along the way. But perhaps more importantly, she has been the source of the patience that I have brought to doing my work day in, day out over the last five-plus decades. I was a corporate lawyer and then a merger and acquisitions specialist—and to be sure, when you're bringing together two companies, you have to have a whole lot of patience.

More than patience, however, you also have to understand who you're dealing with. You have to understand their objectives. What exactly are they trying to do? Are they trying to sell their business because they want to be part of a bigger picture? Are they selling because they have financial problems? Are they selling because the owner is getting older and there is no successor in place? These are all typical reasons for why a company is selling. From a buyer's point of view, you have to know what the company is looking to acquire and why. Are they aiming to go into another field that compliments their own? Are they after geographic expansion? Are they hoping to deploy capital because their existing businesses are flattening out? Are they just sitting on a lot of money and figure that it should be used for expansion? Every situation is a little bit different, but generally speaking, the factors are often quite straight forward. You know it's one of the above, and you don't have to guess. You're either being told a, b, or c, and the information is right there in the numbers.

But this is not always the case, especially with some of these titans of the industry who are, what I may euphemistically call, idiosyncratic. Their idiosyncratic natures often filter down through all aspects of their lives, including their business lives, and this can make it difficult for a person to know why they may wish to sell or buy a company. At this point, to do my job well, I have to become a kind of sleuth or psychiatrist. Yes, a psychiatrist—that's probably more like it. I have to get inside the mind of my client and treat it as if it were an onion, pulling back the layers, one after another, hopefully to some end. And sometimes, when I get all the way in there, I can't believe what I've found. You won't either.

Speaking of being able to understand your clients, one day, Les Wexner, one of the greatest retailers of all time, founder of the Limited Stores, called me up. He knew that I represented Milton Petrie, founder of Petrie Stores Corporation. Les wanted to explore selling all of his Lerner Stores in Puerto Rico and the Virgin Islands to Petrie.

I said, "You do?"

And he told me that he did indeed.

"But why?" I said. These stores were incredibly profitable. In my mind, it was the equivalent of him saying, "Hey, what are you doing today? Any chance we can throw away a couple of great moneymakers? Terrific. I was hoping you'd say so."

Wexner didn't give me any explanation then. He just told me to please get Milton on the phone and see if he was interested in buying the stores.

My confusion notwithstanding, I gave a call to my dear friend Milton Petrie. Milton was what I like to refer to as a Merchant Prince. At the time, he was one of the richest retail magnates in the country. Besides running Petrie Stores, which was a multi-billion-dollar company, he owned 25 percent of Toys "R" Us, which was then an outstanding company. (Upon his passing, at age ninety-two, Milton owned 38 percent of Toys "R" Us stock, valued at a billion and a half dollars.) Milton and I had done deals together, and knowing Milton's business the way I did, I was well aware that his own stores in Puerto

Rico and the Virgin Islands were some of his most successful enterprises with four-wall profits in excess of 25 percent, which is very high in the industry. So, I called Milton on the phone and laid out Wexner's hopes to sell his stores to him. Milton was absolutely interested, but again, like myself, he didn't know why in the world Wexner would hand him so many bags and bags of cash, so to speak. What was the catch?

Milton asked me if Wexner was nuts.

"It's just something he tells me he's got to do," I said.

And so, Milton told me to get the numbers together, and we would take it from there.

I began putting together the information, doing my due diligence. Seeing these explosively lucrative financials behind each of Wexner's Puerto Rico and Virgin Island operations broken down, however, the more I scratched my head and had to acknowledge that this really was an odd set of circumstances. I wanted to call Wexner up and set him straight. But instead, knowing Wexner and really in no position to question him, I did as I was being paid to do, and I brought all the information back to Milton. Milton began to look over the numbers, and then we were looking at them together, the two of us standing behind a table, side by side, and scratching our heads in unison: this was too good to be true. We began to wonder if it *was* too good to be true. Of course, we all know that if something looks too good to be true, it probably is exactly that. But Les Wexner was one of those figures setting the benchmark in retail. He was the new generation, younger than Milton. He was a person with whom I had already done plenty of deals, and he was not trying to pull any funny business on me or the legendary Milton Petrie. What would be his motive in doing that? But then why? Why! Milton and I just couldn't understand what would motivate Wexner to sell such a profitable business. The negotiation went on for three months, four months, and throughout that time we continued to be baffled. Then one day, the truth came to me, and just as we had known all along, none of this had anything at all to do with any malfeasance or dishonesty. No, what it turned out to be was more confusing to us than anything we could have imagined. Wexner was superstitious about operating retail stores outside the continental US. Les Wexner? Superstitious?

Yes. Les Wexner. Superstitious.

The forty-eight states that spanned from sea to shining sea—those were the ones Wexner's gut told him to do business within, and nothing beyond those borders. Why? Les couldn't really explain it to you either. It wasn't based on facts and numbers. It was fully in his head. And honestly, I couldn't believe it. Milton was likewise shocked. "Only the forty-eight states of the continental United States!" Milton said to me over the phone that day. But didn't Wexner realize that the whole world was for the taking?

"He doesn't want to be a part of it," I said to Milton. "Not even Alaska or Hawaii. *Just* the continental US." (Although in later years, Wexner would change his mind about this, he would still miss the opportunity to buy the Body Shop at half the price L'Oréal paid for it. This would have been a most successful acquisition to bring his Bath & Body Works division global.)

Milton was happy to capitalize on Wexner's unusual thinking. But you know, everyone in his and her own way. I wouldn't criticize Wexner or insult his intelligence. After all, despite the hurt to his reputation from his dealings with Jeffrey Epstein, he's one of the most successful retail entrepreneurs to have ever graced the planet, and I was pleased to be doing business with him, no matter the unique geographic constraints he applied to his operation.

With that said, you see why sometimes it can be difficult to figure out the needs of a seller or buyer. You hope it's as simple as looking at the numbers or taking in the larger picture of the industry and seeing where the winds are blowing, and then saying, "Hey, there's room for growth here and here. Let's sell that. Let's acquire that." But when you get into the very big time, with these titans of the industry, you've got to understand who you're dealing with on a deeper level, to learn about who they are, where they've been, what business means to them, and why they do any of it at all. The Milton Petries and Les Wexners of the world are playing the game at a level that goes so far beyond just dollars and cents. They're not just in it for the money, no. They're after something that is so particular, so personal, so utterly...*them.*

And then sometimes they're after something that's not deep at all but something quite astonishingly superficial.

Not long after doing that very deal between Wexner and Milton on the Puerto Rico and Virgin Islands stores, the three of us went out for lunch at the restaurant in the East 60s owned by Milton, Quo Votus—at the time, one of New York's great restaurants. It was a place I used to spend a lot of time with Milton. (No longer there, I do miss it.) On this particular day, Milton began to tell us that he had recently been on Donald Trump's yacht. He said to Wexner that he knew he had a yacht as well, and he asked him how big his yacht was. Wexner said somewhere in the ballpark of two hundred and ten feet. To which Milton replied that Donald's was two hundred and twelve feet. We then continued on with our lunch and eventually said our goodbyes. About two months later, the three of us happened to be together again, and Wexner said to Milton that he had something he had to tell him about his yacht. Milton turned to him, all ears. Wexner told him that his yacht was now two hundred and *eighteen* feet! That's right, since our last get-together, Wexner had added some eight feet to the bow of his yacht so as to surpass the length of Trump's yacht. Needless to say, Wexner had a huge ego. But they all did and do. They couldn't be what they are without the ego and power.

In fact, Trump called me something of an ego-inflating name of my own: "the King of 7th Avenue." Why? Because of all the apparel and retail deals I had done. Trump rang me up one day and asked me over to his office at the top of Trump Towers. He said he'd like me to develop a licensing program for him. And I said, sure. Of course I would. Certainly, I saw the opportunity there, but remember, this was before Donald Trump was a television celebrity with a program of his own and long before any of us could have imagined that he'd go all the way to the White House. Like him or not, he was a figure in New York City real estate with a reputation for leveraging his family name into some successful and some not-so-successful enterprises. Well, I came back to Trump Towers a few weeks later with two or three of my people. We laid out a whole program for him. And, he said that he thought these plans were great and that we should start immediately.

And I said, "Donald, we can start immediately except for one thing: we have to agree upon my fee."

He looked at me and repeated the word "fee," as if he had never heard of it before. Then he asked if I really thought I should be charging him a fee, being that the honor of working for him would bring me more money than a fee would ever bring.

I didn't do the deal.

But there is always a dance involved with any of these merchants. We are here to do business, but we are also here to play out the idea of who we are and who we wish to become. You come across some individuals who are reclining on clouds floating up, up, up, so very close to the sun. I do my best to spend the kind of time where you can really get to know someone. It's not a rush to the finish line. We're all in it for the long haul—certainly I am, anyway—and I like to get on a personal level.

For instance, with Milton Petrie:

I would meet Milton either at his office in Secaucus where this billionaire paid short shrift to his immaculate desk, basically working off a great, long card table so he could review store by store figures back when they were printed on large paper sheets. He knew what every store was doing and what the volume was, up and down. He was a total hands-on person, looking at all the numbers—every number. In those days, before the internet and an advanced computer information structure, he would get stacks and stacks of these printouts. He was a true renegade in apparel retail, having started in Cleveland and building a business out of several small women's apparel stores gone bankrupt. He then restarted and became one of the largest specialty apparel retailers in the country, doing junior clothing. At the time, in the 1970s, I had been doing a lot of retail deals myself, and one sort of built on the other. I had done deals with retail conglomerates including Interco, Brooks Fashion, U.S. Shoe, Edison Brothers, and, more importantly, Melville Corporation. But I began to look more and more for the independent retail companies that were controlled by one or more individuals, and among them, was Petrie Stores Corporation. I met Milton just like I met so many people over the years. I would see these businesses that were very interesting to me, and I'd go after them. I was aggressive; I enjoyed the hunt and chase of finding these people and getting into business with them. Of course, in the beginning, a guy like Milton looked at me as just a broker, a service person. I'm a hired hand, yes, and any other investment banker who thinks differently is wrong.

But Milton knew I was building something. He used to call me often around 7:30 in the morning just to chat, because he had already been awake for a while working. We would occasionally go out to dine with our wives, have drinks at his apartment in the Carlyle, in the same apartment where Jack Kennedy had lived with its 360-degree wraparound views of the city. I told them the story of how I had been an editor on my college newspaper at the University of Pennsylvania, *The Daily Pennsylvanian*, and how my aggressiveness had given me the spunk to call the White House in 1961 after President Kennedy was elected. His press secretary, Pierre Salinger, invited me to come spend a day in the White House and interview the President. I had sat in the Oval Office at a time when it was still easy to do that as far as security was concerned. It was also the day that President Kennedy announced the start of the Peace Corps, which was amazing, and also the first time that Eleanor Roosevelt visited. I walked down the hall with both of them, and my picture appeared in all the newspapers the following day with me between them. When one of my mother's friends saw the picture in the *New York Times*, she said, "Boy, Kennedy has a secret service agent that looks just like your son!" But now I was up in the Carlyle in Kennedy's old apartment with Milton and our wives, having drinks, and telling them that very story. How strange life is. The apartment was small but lovely, and Carol Petrie, Milton's "fourth and last" wife, had done a lot of hunting, and in the foyer, were stuffed heads of lion and deer she had killed. Believe me, they sent a message.

To be sure, I knew that we were there because *this* was *business*, as did Milton. But we nurtured these ties to create a bond and trust that would carry over into the deal-making side of our lives. That was my way, and that was certainly Milton's way as well. You saw it throughout his business and personal life. Milton's lawyer was Joe Flom. He was the very well-known head of Skadden, Arps. Ace Greenberg, who built Bear Stearns up into the company it became, was his stockbroker, and the two of them, along with Larry Tisch, were on his board. They would play bridge together every day at the Regency Bridge Club. Were they there for business? Well, it was certainly not just friendship. They liked one another tremendously, but Joe Flom was embedded with Milton, and when Milton would call him with questions, Joe would take the phone call every single time. Honestly, I couldn't understand why Joe, who was working on the biggest takeover in the world, would stop everything to speak with Milton. I found out after Milton died that Joe was the trustee of his estate, and God knows what Joe made for being a trustee. The estate was valued at over a billion dollars. At one point, Milton thought that he might take over Paul Harris Stores (a company Les Wexner had failed to buy). Milton, being the way he was, went and bought about 10 percent of Paul Harris Stores on the opening market. Now, if you buy over 5 percent of a company's shares, you have to file a 13D with the SEC. Milton had Joe and Skadden Arps file the paperwork. But the filing didn't stipulate whether he was buying the stock for investment purposes or because he intended to own the company. Of course, the stock, in reaction to Milton's moves, went up tremendously. Two weeks later, Milton sold the stock and made a bundle. In ordinary circumstances, this would have been the start of a huge SEC investigation. But because he had Joe Flom on board, nothing happened to Milton. He did the same thing with Deb Shops, another junior apparel company. So, was Joe Flom just a good friend of Milton's? Not quite. But they were able to beautifully walk the line between business and friendship, and their ties were deep.

After Milton died, I was asked by Ace Greenberg to find a buyer for Milton's company. He had not been able to put a successor in place among his family members. When you're seeking a buyer for a company where the head is no longer among the living—and in this case, that person was an absolute legend who had left behind a formidable if downward-trending business—you want to find the very best buyer. Do you feel a little extra pressure to do so? Perhaps. But it's more about the excitement of putting the company on a solid path for years to come. I talked to a lot of people, and I ended up getting Warburg Pincus, who moved to acquire the company. Petrie Stores had been doing well, but the recession hurt the company very badly. It eventually went bankrupt and was sold in pieces. Whether that would have happened anyway with Milton at the helm, who knows. The failure to put a real succession plan in process created a lot of problems. And no question, it had been Milton's genius for retail and his fighting spirit that had kept that business going since 1927. When he passed, no matter who was put in charge, the company wasn't going to be the same, and the chances of it surviving the up-and-down world of retail was going to be drastically reduced. A sad commentary, indeed.

To the founders, these companies are like their babies. Only they can really raise them right. Perhaps it's easier to think about that very statement when put in a slightly different context. Let me mention a different name here, one that's more well-known among households than that of Milton Petrie: Martha Stewart. What will the Martha Stewart brand be when Martha Stewart is no longer with us? Who can do Martha's business better, as well as—or even half as well as—Martha herself?

I first met Martha Stewart at a dinner party shortly after Shelley and I moved to New York in the mid-1980s. I was then at Lehman, and I was the new guy on the block. I was at a dinner party in Westport, Connecticut, at the home of Sam Heyman, who was a true titan of industry. Seated next to me at the table was a woman who introduced herself as Martha Stewart. I introduced myself and she said, "What do you do?" I said that I was an investment banker at Lehman Brothers. Then I said to her, "What do you do?" She looked at me and stared and said, "I'm Martha Stewart," like I was an idiot. Okay, so not everyone knew who Martha Stewart was back then. I certainly didn't. This was just as she was rising to fame with a number of very successful books about cooking, and her name was beginning to appear all over the place in magazines and on television.

She and I would go on to form a very good relationship over time and work on a number of things together. She had grown to become the major licensee at Kmart then. This was true to such a degree that her brand, Martha Stewart, was almost synonymous with the Kmart label. She was doing everything from home products to gardening, and all those creative around-the-house fixes that she seemed to have up her sleeve by the millions. But there was a huge recession in the early-1990s that really hit all the retailers hard, and Kmart started to have problems, and there was a question as to what direction they would take. Chuck Conaway had been made the CEO of Kmart, and he was a talented guy, but Kmart was still a total mess. The complacency of the prior management, run by Floyd Hall, had really brought Kmart down to a new low. I had been working on a number of things with them. In fact, I had become director of Blue Light, which would become Kmart's e-commerce division. It should have been very successful but was not because it was too early in the life of the home computer and e-commerce, and people didn't understand either. Though it was common to work with computers at your office, there was hardly a computer in every home (which is something that in today's world is hard to believe). Kmart spent a lot of money, brought home computers into the stores, and no one bought them. And while Blue Light should have been very successful, it failed. In the meantime, Chuck Conaway was caught in a scandal and left the company, and Kmart was sort of in hiatus.

In this downturn, Martha Stewart saw a great opportunity, and she tried with my help to put together a group of people to takeover Kmart and to use her merchandising insights to bring Kmart back to where it had been in the decades before. Martha also talked to me about working with Sears, who had recently taken over Kmart. The end result is that, while we spent time on it, we were never able to do either. Over the years, I also worked with her on licensing deals to bring her brand to Europe and Asia. It is a shame that she went to jail for a short time, as it really hurt her business. But she certainly is a true survivor.

In a situation like this, there are so many moving parts: the economy, the trends of the industry, the quality and insights of upper-management, and above all else, the mind of a singular entrepreneur like Martha Stewart. She's put so much blood, sweat, and tears into turning her name into this great force known to all. She's the one who's up late and then back at it before sunrise, striving to stay ahead of everyone else and be this formidable brand. As one of the people helping her expand the reach of her brand, we also have to be sensitive to her needs. And those needs are not as simple and straightforward as just numbers indicated on a spreadsheet. You've got to really get inside the minds of people like Martha Stewart and figure out their motivations at the deepest levels. Above all else, remember, it's their name right there on the store, on the package, on the book. They're the ones assuming the most risk. You always have to bear that in mind.

Personally, one of the most satisfying examples of a name brand I helped turn into a globally recognized company was Stuart Weitzman. This was after I had bought back Financo from Lehman. Howard Platt, the former head of U.S. Shoe, told me that I should really talk to Stuart Weitzman, that he was a fantastic operator, he was getting older, and maybe it was time he should consider selling his company. So I set up a meeting and met Stuart. It turned out he had gone to school with my wife, and we had a lot of mutual friends. He ended up retaining Financo to find a home for the company. There was another famous shoe company at the time called Joan & David. They were run by a husband-and-wife team, real entrepreneurs, who, as they got older, for one reason or another, started fighting, and their business fell apart. They had partnered with Ann Taylor, and it became a major part of the Ann Taylor operation, but that ended. I mention Joan & David here because Stuart Weitzman was almost the complete opposite to them as far as his own needs: he only wanted to sell to a strategic buyer who would allow him to keep his organization intact and continue to grow the company and give a lot of input. So, right away, that takes a lot of companies right off the table and puts me onto a very specific kind of search.

The first two companies we targeted were Coach and Burberry. The reason we chose them was that Stuart felt his expertise in the shoe business could absolutely benefit Burberry, which had done some footwear that he knew needed to be updated. Coach wasn't in the footwear business—they were in handbags—but perhaps they were ready to expand into the footwear business. Unfortunately, neither Coach nor Burberry were interested in buying Stuart Weitzman. Burberry wanted to stay a single-branded company, owning nothing other than the one Burberry name. And Coach felt Stuart Weitzman was too small for them to buy. If they were going to do an acquisition, it was going to be a billion-dollar deal, not one for hundreds of millions. Stuart was doing so well, and he really loved his business, but naturally he was disappointed that neither company bit. We then talked to a number of other people. I called the CEO of Brown Shoe, another retail conglomerate. They were extremely interested and willing to pay a lot of money. They came to a meeting with a huge replica of a Stuart Weitzman box inside of which were Chanel and Louis Vuitton products, among others. Despite their efforts, Stuart didn't like the chemistry, and he decided it wouldn't be a good match. Next, we went to speak to a few private equity firms. I convinced Stuart that a private equity firm would not only give him a lot of money but would also help him grow and develop the business into a bigger company that could then be sold. We ended up talking to John Howard, who at the time was head of Bear Stearns Merchant Banking. John and his partner, Richard Perkal, fell in love with Stuart Weitzman. We ended up structuring a deal where they bought forty-something percent and allowed Stuart to absolutely run the company. I even joined the board of the company. At the original closing dinner, Stuart presented Richard with a pair of women shoes and had him parade around the dining room at the Four Seasons. A real sight to behold! Anyway, Stuart continued to grow, but after two or three years it became obvious that Bear Stearns wanted to sell the company. And right like that, we were back at it. We talked to a number of people, like the Burberrys again, and they still weren't interested. We ended up selling to Jones Apparel, who I knew because I had sold to them Gloria Vanderbilt Jeans, among other companies. Jones also owned 9 West, which was also in the footwear business. Jones bought 51 percent of Stuart Weitzman and let Stuart keep 49 percent. And although Jones gave him total independence, the chemistry was never quite there, and the deal didn't work out the way it should have. Even so, a year or two later, Jones Apparel ended up buying the balance of the business—and each time Stuart made a whole lot of money. Jones was then taken over by Sycamore, and they put the Stuart Weitzman brand up for sale. I was not involved in the sale, but, if you can believe it, Coach swept in and ended up buying Stuart Weitzman. So, in the end, Coach *was* interested. Unfortunately, they've totally ruined Stuart's company, losing $50 million last year and having written off the entire investment of over $700 million. Today, Stuart Weitzman is a small division of Coach, maybe 2 or 3 percent of its sales. You just never know how these deals are going to go. So much of it comes down to timing and to who's running the show. Is it hard to watch a longtime friend see the company he built—his baby, yes—be acquired and then taken down in flames by the next parent? Well, I like to remind him: "Look, you've made a lot of money." And now he's using some of those many millions to increase a worldwide commitment to Jewish causes. He's building the first museum in Spain about the Jewish Diaspora, from which he is a descendent. Finally, Stuart can often be found teaching at universities, especially at the University of Pennsylvania where the Design School is named after him. If you ask me, I'd say it's all worked out.

Gilbert with Marvin Traub at a WWD CEO Conference.

CHAPTER 2

The Great Lion of the Industry: My Years Alongside the Legendary Marvin Traub

YOU MEET A LOT OF people along the way. And if you're someone like myself who tries to get in front of everyone and is more than game to fly around the world to have a face to face with an entrepreneur and learn just what his business is all about, you're quite possibly going to come across some of the greatest people the industry has to offer. I've mentioned some who fit that description already. And yet it's hard to believe that I'm all these pages along and I've yet to mention Marvin.

Marvin who?

Marvin Traub, of course. He was an absolute legend of the industry and whom I would call the ultimate Merchant Prince.

As a lover of retail and merchandising, a tough boss, highly demanding, Marvin did nothing less than recreate Bloomingdale's and build it up significantly in the 1970s and 1980s. There's a reason why the name alone—Bloomingdale's—has that very special ring to it. Yes, you hear it said and your eyes and ears perk up, and you start to feel just a little bit more alive. That is because of the brilliant work Marvin did there. (After Marvin's retirement, Michael Gould came in as the CEO and built Bloomingdale's into an even greater store.)

I met Marvin around 1982 under what, for him, were unusual circumstances. At the time, Marvin was approaching sixty-five, which was the mandatory retirement age at Federated (the owner of Bloomingdale's). Now, I don't like to use the word retirement. I know it's there in the dictionary between "no way" and "not me." Actually, it's a word people like myself and Marvin don't have in our vocabularies. We don't like to hear it said, and we bristled anytime someone dared to use it about one of us. Marvin, in his early sixties, was in his prime, at the top of his game, and on a winning streak: the 1970s had been a tremendous time for Bloomingdale's. Receipts were up, but also, the image of the store was exploding. Who could forget Marvin walking Queen Elizabeth and Prince Philip through those sacred halls on 59th Street in 1976? Or, two years later, the new restaurant, Le Train Bleu, going in upstairs, a reproduction of the same train car you'd take when traveling through France on your way from Lyon to Monte Carlo? Or the flags that had been installed on the outside of the building of nations from all around the world, as if Bloomingdale's was its own little United Nations? (It's fair to say that Marvin knew globalization was the future well before any of us did.) Still, rules being rules, Marvin would have to leave the company and retire. This was something he absolutely did not want to do. But no one at Federated was making any noise about it. In fact, no one was even talking about it. But certainly, there was this huge disruption on the horizon, and it was preoccupying Marvin.

Marvin and I were speaking about the circumstances one afternoon and wondering what steps could be taken with regards to his future. If you're me in that moment, it's like you're talking to Mickey Mantle coming off an MVP season, his contract is up, and you're asking the slugger what's next. To be sure, there's so much opportunity, but what is the right next step?

For one thing, we knew that B Altman was coming on the market because the company had lost significant market share. B Altman was a large department store with about ten to fifteen locations in the Northeast, and it was very intriguing. B Altman was smaller than Bloomingdale's but could have had the same pizzaz with Marvin and the people who worked for him running the company. We went to sleep on it and woke up inspired. A few weeks later, after looking through the numbers and talking it all over, Marvin and I approached B Altman's banker with the idea that he would buy the company. We had a small fund back then, and Victor Barnett, the former chairman of Burberrys, was my partner in it. He was intrigued as well. Even if you're as well informed as Marvin and I, however, before you do something this big, you want to get as much expert advice as you can. You have to open your ears and listen to what people in the know have to say. So, we went to talk to Larry Tisch, who was a close friend of Marvin's, and a person I knew from my dealings with Milton Petrie. Larry was a veritable giant of the industry. He saw how B Altman had a ton of real estate on the books, and while we thought it was extremely valuable, Larry told us that we shouldn't do it because New York was falling apart and our investment would be worth nothing. It's a moment that sits with you and expands, bigger, bigger, in your heart and mind. Larry Tisch is Larry Tisch, and when he says something, you have to respect it. And ultimately, you probably have to listen to him.

Marvin and I didn't listen. We said that we would do it regardless. We'd takeover B Altman and have a great time showing the world what a terrific department store it could be, bringing in the finest people, the greatest products, and really showcasing how a product should be sold in that kind of retail space. And our downside was protected with the real estate which was still very valuable. We were thrilled, exhilarated. I saw my next years laid out before me. I would be with Marvin, taking on a whole new beast. I was ready.

There were no contracts drawn up yet, and certainly no drying ink to mention. But Marvin had to tell his new plan to Howard Goldfeder, the CEO of Federated, and hearing this, *he* went bananas. *He* was not going to lose Marvin Traub. And perhaps more importantly, he was not going to allow this Merchant Prince to become a competitor in New York, New Jersey, and Connecticut. And why? Just because he was about to turn sixty-five? Sixty-five was the new forty-five. Heck, it was the new forty! Hadn't everyone heard? Howard called a special meeting of the board of directors at Federated and increased the retirement age to seventy, just like that, one, two, three. Marvin was pleased. He didn't want to leave behind Bloomingdale's. After all, he had done so much for the company, and he wasn't done.

To my great unhappiness, with Marvin set to remain at Bloomingdale's, our deal with B Altman died, and what I got out of it in terms of payment for the deal that never happened was a dinner at La Bernadin. One of my favorite restaurants in town, but I'm afraid to say that on that particular evening, the meal didn't taste quite as delicious as it usually did. I was upset, frustrated. But then, it's hard to know what fruits may come of an experience like the one I had just been through until long afterwards. Sitting in that Michelin-starred Midtown dining room, I couldn't know what was to be the future for me and Marvin. But we had just been through a lot together, and we had learned a lot about one another, and we liked what we saw.

Marvin and I stayed in close touch. Shelley and I got to know his wife, Lee. And, about four years later, after a great run at Bloomingdale's in the mid-1980s, having opened new stores in California and Florida and Texas, and having brought in the Bloomingdale's charge card and cemented his relationship with all the biggest designers of the day—especially Ralph Lauren, as well as Calvin Klein, Donna Karan, Georgio Armani, and of course with the Estee Lauder Company where Leonard Lauder and Marvin were very close—Marvin did indeed retire from Bloomingdale's and set up his own consulting firm. He seemed busy, happy with his work. But one day we were having lunch and I said to him, "Marvin, why don't you join us at Financo? You would become the Senior Advisor. You'd use all of your contacts. You'd bring in business, and it will be a great opportunity."

Now, you have to understand, Marvin could get ahold of any person in the world. While I could get ahold of a whole *lot* of people, Marvin was unbelievable and had a great contact list. You just couldn't believe his Rolodex—and you can be sure that no one ever sent him to voicemail. To have him at Financo would be tremendous, the kind of thing you reach for at a strategic moment on the basis of a gut feeling and nothing more, hoping to hear that magic word: yes. To my enormous satisfaction, Marvin *said* yes. And, thinking back to the B Altman deal that had fallen apart just a few years prior and how much that had hurt, it was something to find myself here all of a sudden, with Marvin, the two of us about to embark on a whole new great journey—one that would in all probability allow us a lot more freedom to do what we liked when and how we liked without the demands of running a department store and the pressures of keeping its business prospering. This was going to be truly fun, a new great adventure. I was over the moon.

We gave Marvin the big office. His assistant, Amy Hafkin, was a fantastic presence in the office. Marvin had the title of Senior Advisor, and he had his name and title put on the door: Marvin Traub Consultants under the Financo nameplate and logo. Honestly, that posed a bit of a conflict with some people at the office, because Marvin's was now the only door with a name and a title on it. But we worked around it. And Marvin was a force—you wanted to please him and give him what he needed to be Marvin Traub. He was helping me solicit clients, and there were certain situations—the kind I'd been trying to get across the finish line for years—that Marvin really pushed us over the top on. What do I mean? Well, take Liz Claiborne's purchase of Ellen Tracy, for instance. I knew Herb Gallen, the founder and CEO of Ellen Tracy, which was one of the major bridge apparel companies located in New York. I almost sold his company once, but the deal hadn't happened. Why? It's hard to say. Of course, getting a founder to sell can be very tricky. Their companies are their babies, their lifeblood. It's the very thing that gets them up and going every morning.

But now Marvin and I were able to go to Herb together and really get him to see the reality. Which was that Herb was getting older, and while his business was doing extremely well now, who really knew about tomorrow and the years to come. He had his own plane, a two-hundred-foot yacht. Did he need for more? Definitely not. After a lifetime of business, this was the prime moment for him to cash out. And Marvin really helped push Herb over that hump. I had been trying for a while, to no avail. Here comes Marvin and he pushes all the right buttons. How does he do it? Is it something he says? Some wisdom? Some grain of truth? Fact was, I had probably used all the same words as Marvin to try and encourage Herb to sell the company. So no, it was not in the pitch. It was just in Marvin being Marvin. At this point in his career, Marvin could accomplish so much just by sheer presence alone—and we sold the business for a lot of money.

But above all else, Marvin just worked extremely hard.

I remember in those days, the early to mid-1990s, the power breakfast was at the Regency, and everybody who was anybody would be there. Except for one thing: if you really had something confidential to do, you didn't go there. Same with the Grill Room at the Four Seasons. Both were places where Marvin and I would go regularly to solicit and talk and entertain people. If you wanted to ensure that no one heard your sensitive information, you did not go to either of these places. But Marvin called me up one morning and said we had a 7:30 breakfast at the Regency. I replied, "Marvin, I can't do it. I have my trainer from seven to eight."

But then he told me to do what *he* did: have your trainer come at six in the morning. This, from a guy who was fifteen years older than me. His energy and stamina were unbelievable. We used to go to Europe on the Concorde. We'd arrive in Paris, check in at our hotel—Marvin always liked to stay at the Crillon, I liked the Ritz or the Bristol, but while with him we'd always stay at the Crillon—and Marvin would want to have a meeting fifteen minutes later. I'd like to rest and catch my breath a minute. But that was his stamina. It was incredible. We were always flying one place or another, the two of us. We didn't stop.

There was a trip Marvin and I took to Hong Kong when we began working with David Tang. Tang was one of the serial entrepreneurs there. Besides owning the China Club, which was an institution in Hong Kong, he had started Shanghai Tang—a department store in Shanghai and Beijing that sold unbelievable goods developed by the company. But Hermes was opening a store in Hong Kong, and they had asked David to welcome their brand into this new market by hosting a very high-end fashion show in Hong Kong. David invited Marvin and I, along with our wives, to attend the event. Of course, we said yes. And after arriving in Hong Kong, David asked us out to his house on the water—which was just spectacular—with all of Hong Kong springing up right before you and the boats and this wonderful new world for us. There were about ten of us there for lunch, including Shelley and myself, Marvin and his wife, Lee, David Tang and his fiancée, Jean-Louis Dumas, who was the head of Hermes, and his son, Pierre-Alexis Dumas. We had a phenomenal luncheon at this seaside house of Tang's, and all during the luncheon, the elder Dumas was scribbling in a notebook. He'd look up at me, make a small little drawing. Then his eyes would dart over to Marvin or Lee or Shelley, and he'd do another sketch of one of them in his notebook or draw a picture of the boats passing along in the water. (Some months later, back home in New York, we received the latest Hermes catalog, and on every page was the doodling that Jean-Louis had done that day.) Fortunately, I had been wearing plenty of Hermes. Well, we had our meetings with David and Shanghai Tang, attended a tremendous fashion show, and all was going very well between us. Then, on the third night, the China Club had a huge gala for Hermes with about two to three hundred people under a tent down near the water. Believe it or not, the ceiling of this tent was lined with the same patterned leather used on the Hermes bag. So, as you could imagine, no expense was being spared by the company. They wanted to make an impact, and they were doing exactly that. In fact, after this elaborate dinner, we went down to the sea to watch a sailboat with the Hermes flags flapping in the wind and a phenomenal fireworks display. I mean, what next? When the sailboat had passed and the fireworks came to an end, we went back to the table to sit down and there were these tremendous orange Hermes boxes at our seats. Shelley was ecstatic. She said, "Can you believe it? They're going to give us a pocketbook!" She opened up the box and inside was a crystal copy of the very sailboat we had just seen passing along the water (a gift which I still have in my office). Next, we flew to Shanghai for the Hermes store opening and then over to Beijing for another Hermes opening, all of which was very interesting. Marvin and I had seen a lot in our time, but this felt like something different. It *was* something different. It was an enormous market on the other side of the world that was reaching out to us. And the bottom line of the visit was that David Tang retained us to bring Shanghai Tang to the United States. This was a big deal—a giant in the Chinese market bringing his brand to New York for the first time. And he had chosen us to do it. We were thrilled.

Back in New York, Marvin and I secured unbelievable space for Shanghai Tang in Leonard Stern's building at 62nd and Madison. The vision was to start with a store on the ground floor. We reserved space on the second floor as well where David Tang could do a China Club restaurant and tie the two locations together, which would have been phenomenal. But, one step at a time. First, we had to open the Shanghai Tang store and set that business into motion. This was a very exciting proposition, especially with Marvin there to steer David in putting together a successful retail space in New York. *That* was Marvin's specialty. With all of this firepower, we were feeling optimistic. And why shouldn't we have been? A lot of work had gone into this moment, and there was tremendous buzz and excitement around the arrival of this great Chinese brand landing on Madison Avenue. Richemont, the Swiss luxury goods brand, was a major shareholder in Shanghai Tang, and the chairman came to New York for the opening. We were having breakfast with him in the penthouse of the Four Seasons Hotel the morning of the opening. He was smoking a cigar, as some people are inclined to do at 8:00 a.m., and he set off the fire alarm and the entire hotel had to be evacuated. A bad omen? I don't know. I don't look for signs. But breakfast was ruined, yes. That night, the city closed off Madison Avenue at 62nd Street, and there were hundreds of people trying to get into the event. Because of the crowds, it was difficult to physically get inside, and Johann Rupert, the CEO of Richemont—one of the hosts of the evening—was almost unable to get in. We had a great night though. Everyone was feeling very hopeful about the future of the store and where we might go from there as far as further expansion into the US market. And well, the store *should* have done exceptional business. Unfortunately, it didn't. Why? The reason was not especially complicated. In the end, David wouldn't listen to Marvin's merchandising advice, which was why he had hired us in the first place. Take this detail, for instance, which may come across as very small and insignificant but is really quite important: David only wanted to have pink, yellow, red, and blue towels in the store. Marvin kept telling him that 70 percent of all towels sold in the United States were white, and while you can have all the colors, you've still got to have white towels as well. David refused. When you went into the store in Hong Kong there were picture frames and other items you could buy for twenty to a hundred dollars, which would have been great house gifts. He didn't have these in the New York location. Meanwhile, he was pushing the colored bathrobes and the Chinese suits and clothing, which just weren't right for the time and the place. New York is its own animal. You've got to know how to attend to it. And where we all have to go on our instincts—entrepreneurs perhaps more than anyone—when you're struggling and have someone like Marvin diagnosing the problem and spelling out the cure, you have little choice but to listen to him. In all likelihood, he's right and you, no matter how much success you've had, are wrong. But David wouldn't listen, and he *was* wrong. The store did poorly, and it closed.

It was disappointing. We maintained our friendship with David, and he would see us when he came to New York. But it was not the same.

In time, Marvin, too, departed Financo. We had done wonderful things together, and I'm sure we would have done even more. But Marvin's ego pushed him to concentrate solely on Marvin Traub Associates. There were no hard feelings. We had ten productive years together. His insights and the mentorship he gave me were unparalleled and something I will forever hold dear. Sadly, Marvin got kidney cancer, and in July of 2012 at the age of eighty-seven, he passed away. In the first paragraph of his obituary in the *New York Times*, it said that he had "transformed Bloomingdale's from a stodgy Upper East Side family department store into a trendsetting international showcase of style and showmanship." The paper of record also referred to him as "one of the most creative retailers of his era." "We are not only in competition with other stores, but with the Guggenheim and the Met," he was quoted as saying. And it mentioned how "Grace Mirabella, *Vogue*'s editor in chief in the 1970s and '80s, anointed him 'the Sol Hurok of retailing,' a reference to the great impresario who brought the Bolshoi Ballet to America." This was a beautiful tribute to a very special person I was fortunate to spend so much time with and to call a great friend.

Gilbert with Tommy Hilfiger at the World Retail Conference
where Tommy was inducted into the Retail Hall of Fame.

CHAPTER 3

The Future Is Now:
How a Deal's Life Depends
on a Company's Willingness
to Grow with the Times

OVER THE PAST FIFTY YEARS, I've worked on hundreds, maybe thousands of deals, first as a lawyer and then as an investment banker and financial advisor. As you might imagine, not every deal works out. I wish I could tell you they did, that every one of them landed just where I hoped. But no, that's not true, nor would it be possible. Is it easy when a deal fails to come through? Sometimes yes. Sometimes no. But of the deals that didn't work out, perhaps the most frustrating aspect, the thing that continues to bother me to this day, sometimes decades after the fact, concerns the deals that really should have happened but didn't because of an owner or C-suite executive's lack of vision to even explore the label. Those individuals sitting across the table from me who were only thinking of the business in the short term or were blind to what was happening in their industry or were stubborn or even worse, lazy, not wanting a challenge. Yes, when I think of the deals that failed because of bad leadership at the top of a company, it hurts me still.

Oftentimes these executives were just afraid. Afraid of what? Failure, naturally, and the possibility of being shown the door in the aftermath of a deal that didn't bring big results. Or else second- or third-level executives didn't want to do anything to upset their hold on power and decided instead to latch onto the status quo as if it were some kind of lifeboat. (Let me tell you, it is almost never the lifeboat they believed it would be.)

Of all the deals that didn't come across the finish line, though, what really irritated me then—and does still—were the executives who thought that I was pushing an idea simply to earn my fee. Look, don't hate me: I like my fee. But first and foremost, I'm passionate about what I do, and what's most important in a deal is that it's successful for the company in the years to come. To see that a deal has caused a company to thrive well into the future is a beautiful thing, and as far as my work goes, is probably the greatest source of satisfaction.

But more often than not, a deal fails because someone at the top can't see the future of the industry. Now, it can seem complicated to know where the winds are blowing in an industry. But I believe the future is usually staring you right in the face and that many people in power choose to look the other way. Think, if you were in the horse and buggy business producing carriages, you should have been smart enough to go into automobiles. And if you owned and operated trains, you should have been right there investing in airplanes. But consider how many people in that position didn't do anything. Think of all the people who said, "No, no. We're in horse and buggies! That's what we do." Or, "No, no. We're in the railroad game! That's us. That's who we are and who we'll always be!"—and they perished because of it. When you see change coming, you can't resist. You have to leap in and embrace it.

What you learn being around a person like Marvin Traub is just how critical it is to be constantly evolving. Interestingly enough, in our time, Marvin and I were able to both witness the rise and significant fall of the department store. And, unsurprisingly, central to its collapse was the failure of department store CEOs to think imaginatively and see the future that was unfolding right before them.

THE GROWTH AND CHANGE OF DEPARTMENT STORES

In the mid- to late-1980s, many of the real estate titans thought they could be as good at running department stores as they were at developing new properties with the department store serving as their own tenant. As a result, I represented Hooker, which was the very successful Australian real estate group that went after B Altman and Bonwit Teller, among others (all of which eventually failed). The Taubman Companies went after Wanamakers in Washington DC. Simon DeBartolo was going to buy Allied Stores, but they were beaten out by Robert Campeau, the Canadian real estate developer who had his eyes on the US retail department store market. Campeau didn't even own any department stores in Canada, but he thought the US market gave him an opportunity to grow.

Campeau first targeted Allied Department Stores and bought them. Before the ink had dried on the contract, he sold off two of Allied's best specialty chains: Ann Taylor, and Brooks Brothers. Bruce Wasserstein represented Campeau and did all of his work, and Bruce really understood the retail sector very well. I was at Lehman. We were representing Allied. Campeau got roughly $600 million for Ann Taylor and another $600 million for Brooks Brothers. This allowed him to pay down a lot of debt and free up money to buy another department store. The next one in his sights was Federated, which at the time was the largest department store company. It was a well-publicized takeover attempt. The press was not very positive; there was little support for it. Federated was trying to fight off Campeau as best as they could.

Les Wexner called me up one day around this time and said that he had an idea to save Federated, and he asked me to set up a meeting for him to talk with Howard Goldfeder, who, as already mentioned, was the chairman and CEO of Federated.

Now, Wexner didn't have just any idea. It was forward thinking with implications on where the department store might find younger customers to keep them growing for years to come. Wexner was willing to offer $250 million into Federated. The way the investment would be structured could prevent Campeau from taking over the business. (Under this arrangement, Campeau would have to pay Wexner a large sum of money if Campeau succeeded in buying Federated.) However, what Wexner wanted in return from Federated was very smart, maybe even brilliant. He asked to put Limited Stores—at the time Wexner's main business and at the height of its success—into Federated Department Stores. Wexner requested about five thousand feet of real estate, give or take. Wexner was ready to pay to have ten shop-in-shops within the department stores refurbished at his expense to test this out. Is that all? No. To top it all off, after eighteen months, should the deal not work out, Wexner would pay to restore the Federated Departments Stores to where they had been before he'd come and put down his footprint. Federated had maybe two hundred stores in the country, but Wexner only wanted to test this idea out in perhaps ten of them.

So, on Wexner's request, I got Howard Goldfeder on the phone and explained the idea to him. Goldfeder seemed intrigued. He told me he would be in touch shortly.

Wexner and I felt confident. After all, Federated was in serious trouble. We thought they needed a way out of the Campeau takeover. And this was not only that; it was a path forward in the aftermath of it all, the creation of a new model of doing business and generating significant investment—both inside and outside the "tent."

Wexner had a private lunch with Goldfeder to explore the idea. A couple of weeks later, Howard came back to us and said that he had looked at all of Federated's real estate—some two hundred department stores around the country—and he had concluded that they just didn't have room in any of their stores to try out Wexner's idea. No room? Really? We were only after space in ten of their roughly two hundred locations around the county, and most of the Federated Stores had between one hundred and three hundred thousand square feet of space. But still, "no" was the answer.

Wexner and I were both shocked. This was a fantastic offer. But, as often happens, it was a fantastic offer that the company just wasn't interested in. Maybe it was because Federated had its own bottom line as far as junior apparel which was Limited's main business then. And maybe Goldfeder really wanted to sell rather than build and stay independent. I really can't say for sure. For me, however, the larger issue—the one that bothers me still—was that if you're Federated, you have the future of your business bearing down on you. You need to go after it, but instead you're showing a total lack of imagination and ingenuity. If you're me, you're wondering what good can come for a company if the people at the very top aren't willing to see the changes that are on the horizon—the change that is already here. A moment like this leaves you with a very bad feeling, and you don't forget it. Especially not when the whole business comes crashing down in the years to come, which was exactly what happened to Federated.

It is interesting to note that what happened to Federated was similar to what would happen shortly after with Macy's and Les Wexner. Wexner still wanted to make a big acquisition, and I brought up acquiring Macy's. The company was having a lot of trouble at the time, and I thought it would be a perfect fit with the Limited. As the Wall Street reporter, Jeffrey Trachtenberg, in his book *The Rain on Macy's Parade: How Greed, Ambition, and Folly Ruined America's Greatest Store*, said, "Wexner couldn't decide whether he wanted to buy Macy's outright or make a similar investment with an option to acquire Macy's at a later date."

Trachtenberg goes onto say that, "The most heated discussions centered on who would lead the companies, Wexner or [Macy's chairman, Edward] Finkelstein...Then the business press got wind of the talks and the talks were over."

Going back to the Federated saga, Goldfeder once told me that one of the biggest mistakes he ever made at Federated was not buying Walmart. But really, the way Federated operated, the company wouldn't have *been* Walmart if Federated had bought them. Walmart has always had its finger on the pulse of the industry. They've always seen the future and helped usher it in (perhaps something written into the DNA of the Walton Family).

Campeau eventually went bankrupt, and Federated brought in Allen Questrom to become Chairman and CEO. Allen had great wisdom on merchandising and was going to bring a whole new face to the business. He also had vision. He took a look at how to grow the business and set his target on Macy's. Macy's had had big problems and was also in bankruptcy. Allen's vision was to buy Macy's and expand it. Macy's was already a national label with stores across the entire country. But his vision was to consolidate all of the Federated labels into a Macy's national banner. This was a brilliant move: making many of the family-owned department stores into one national brand. As a result, if there's anything that is Allen Questrom's legacy, it was taking all of these individual companies and putting them together under one flagship that would give them national recognition. The combined companies thrived over the years. But, as business changed, unfortunately Federated didn't expand further into other areas as consumers became more focused on specialty stores and power malls. This was a frustration that I had. For instance, Federated owned Gold Circle Stores. This was a value-driven department store, a great business. But in 1988, with some seventy-five locations in operation, they sold Gold Circle Stores to Kohl's. (It was the previous management of Federated who had made this decision.) At the time, it might have seemed like the right thing to do. It wasn't. The whole retail industry was heading outside the malls. Kohl's knew that. They were looking around at the trends; they saw the future. Federated could have been

Kohl's if they'd been more imaginative. They'd be doing value, using products outside of the malls on strips and free standing with stores like Gold Circle. But they were stuck in their ways. Look today at the value of Kohl's and compare it to Macy's. They wouldn't evolve. Years later, the CFO of Macy's asked me to acquire all of Kohl's, and of course, it never happened.

Similarly, I tried to get Federated interested in buying some of the growing big box companies, including Bed Bath & Beyond and Linens 'n Things. Domestics was about 9 percent or 10 percent of the department store business. People were going out to the strip centers to buy products. Linens 'n Things and Bed Bath & Beyond were doing very well. I thought Federated should be buying these companies, but they wouldn't act on it. In the deal-making business, you have ideas all the time to grow a company that make total sense, but you're outvoted. If the CEO doesn't have an interest or vision in doing it, they turn you down. Sadly, this results in the demise of the company. It absolutely did at Federated.

Meanwhile, Kohl's was doing better and better. I had become friendly with the management there. Morgan Stanley, which owned approximately 40 percent of Kohl's, was pressuring the management to go public. But Kohl's management, who also owned approximately 40 percent of the company, really didn't want to do it. They liked Kohl's operating just as it was. But after some time, they opened up to the idea. And so, myself and Jeff Branman (who was then one of my people) met with Kohl's management, who authorized us to talk quietly with three companies. First, we spoke with Walmart. Sam Walton had passed away, but I knew his son Rob who was now the chairman. Our idea was that if you put a Walmart at one end of a shopping center and a Kohl's at the other, you'd own the customer. But that didn't materialize. Rob was intrigued but ultimately decided not to go forward because Walmart, at the time, was building superstores, and Rob felt that owning Kohl's would be in conflict with that venture. So, then we talked to Stanley Goldstein, the CEO of the Melville

Corporation, but they thought Bob's, which has since gone bankrupt, was a better box than Kohl's. After Melville turned it down, I called up both Sumner Feldberg and Ben Cammarata, the Chairman and the CEO respectively at TJX, to see if they'd be interested. They went out to meet the Kohl's people, and again nothing happened. So, the three logical companies had all turned Kohl's down. Any of them could have bought Kohl's for around $400 million. Soon after, Kohl's went public at a billion dollars. And when Jay Baker, who was the president of Kohl's, gave $20 million to Wharton—he was on the Wharton board with me—he laughed and said:

> "I was able to give this $20 million to Wharton because you didn't sell the company."

I laughed too. But honestly, it wasn't all that funny to me. The whole industry was moving outside the mall onto the strip center, and it's frustrating because you're trying to get the companies to see this. You're standing there celebrating a $20 million gift, but you're hurting because you're thinking about the companies that didn't listen to you. In particular, with a company like Federated—you're practically waving red flags in their offices, and they still won't listen. And of course, if you're me, you know because nothing was done, the ship went down. Department stores continued to consolidate and consolidate, losing market share all the while. And unfortunately, if you look today at where Macy's was in terms of being the dominant force that they were a number of years ago, it makes you sad. Indeed, it's altogether sad to see the demise of the department stores and the loss of its dominance in the United States over the last fifty years.

At a presentation that I gave in London in 2014 at the annual meeting of the International Association of Department Stores, I reported that, in 1955, there were close to eighty different department store groups operating in the US. Sixty years later, there were only fourteen and today, only eleven. Consolidation, bankruptcy, and liquidation—they happened because of lack of vision and leadership but also because of the rise of the general merchandise stores, discount stores, and the specialty and big box stores. The statistics on the downward trend are amazing. At its peak, the combined market share of department stores in the US was 37.5 percent. By the time I delivered my presentation in London, that figure had decreased to 11.5 percent. All department store revenue combined then totaled $166 billion, while the general merchandise stores had grown to a $67 billion industry—and most amazing was the revenue of the discount stores, which now totaled $655.4 billion, outpacing all other forms of retail. These numbers did not include the specialty stores and mom-and-pop retailers. And now, they continue on their downward cycle, especially with the rise of e-commerce, with Amazon being the leader, with Walmart and Target growing, and many other individually operated standalone e-commerce companies. Certainly, you had the growth of omni-channel retailing which includes both the physical stores and e-commerce ("bricks and clicks"). Unfortunately, none of the department stores knew how to move into the next generation of e-commerce (with the exception, perhaps, of Nordstrom, which has done an exceptional job in building their e-commerce business. Today, it is close to 50 percent of their total revenue). I truly believe department stores fell because they did not invest in the new retail—whether it was in off-price retailing, strip centers, specialty stores, or, of course, e-commerce.

An interesting path forward for one department store in particular was that of Alexander's, the once-successful, mid-level enterprise in the New York/New Jersey area. My own relationship with Alexander's covered several different phases of my life.

While practicing law at Mermelstein in New York City during the earliest stage of my career in the 1960s, Alexander's was a key client of ours, and Milton Mermelstein, the head of the firm, also had a role as the Chairman of Alexander's: Alexander Farkas, who founded and controlled the company, wanted a lawyer on board as chairman. Because of their relationship, I had regular interactions with the company back when it was an extremely well-known department store with its flagship store on the square block one street south of Bloomingdale's on Lexington and Third Avenue between 58th and 59th Street. (Today, it's the site today of the Bloomberg Tower, but more on that in just a bit.)

Fast forward some twenty years to 1990 when Financo was again an independent firm following our years with Lehman. At that time, Alexander's had lost its luster and was on the verge of bankruptcy. The company, though still run by the Farkas Family, was now controlled by three different groups: the strong real estate company, REIT/Vornado, headed by Steve Roth, owned approximately one third of the company; Donald Trump owned approximately another third, although his shares were about to be foreclosed to Citicorp to whom he was indebted; and the balance was owned by the Farkas Family and the public. Steve Roth, a good friend of mine and someone who had built up REIT/Vornado into a formidable name in real estate, loved retail, and in later years he would try to buy JC Penney as well as other retail properties. (Indeed, his position with Alexander's was yet another of those situations where a real estate figure was trying to grow his business by buying up retail.)

One day, Steve called me up and asked to meet with the Alexander's board to discuss a potential engagement to sell Alexander's since the company's stock was sinking. Being retained, we put together the information and a list of buyers that we thought would have a legitimate interest. High at the top of our list was Federated. Our reasons were these: Bloomingdale's was owned by Federated, and Federated was having difficult discussions with the Bloomingdale Trust over the property and the renegotiation of their lease. My thought was that by buying Alexander's, with their flagship location directly next door, Federated would protect themselves in case the new lease couldn't be negotiated. Should that happen, when the existing lease expired, Federated could just go ahead and build a new Bloomingdale's on the Alexander's locations at 58th Street. And the deal would have been to move Sterns (their New Jersey-based department store) into what would then be vacant space in the old Alexander's store. Two things happened next: One, Federated's board turned down the deal since they had just come out of bankruptcy; the press was rumoring this deal, and they were not enjoying the attention the circumstances were bringing. And two, the Bloomingdale's Trust renegotiated Federated's lease. Perhaps this was because of the threat of their buying Alexander's and moving one block south. Who knows?

But our hunt for a buyer for Alexander's continued.

Next on my list was Jay Schottenstein. He was a client of mine. (I would later become an advisor as well as a board member of one of his companies, American Eagle Outfitters.) Among other properties, he controlled Value City Department Stores, and he also loved real estate. Unfortunately, he decided not to pursue Alexander's. I then went to Monroe Milstein, who controlled Burlington Coat Factory, which, at the time, was a very successful company. He also took a serious look at Alexander's and decided to pass.

Having failed to find a buyer and with the company's stock steadily dropping in the interim (to a low of about six dollars a share), Alexander's was headed towards bankruptcy. Today, bankruptcy is considered a vehicle to clean up a company internally and then get it back on the road. But in those days, bankruptcy was thought of as the final stage in a company's demise and not good for your reputation as a businessperson. Boy, have things changed. Filing for bankruptcy was the last thing that Steve Roth wanted, but there was no other alternative, and the company filed, and Alexander's was liquidated. In the process of the selloff, Steve and REIT/Vornado came in and bought most of the stock at this new low price. Steve had the vision to know what the real estate was worth. He sold off the other Alexander's stores but kept the 58th Street property and even demolished the building, creating a real eyesore of a vacancy for years to come. But Roth said he would wait and wait until the right opportunity came along. Eventually, that right opportunity did come along, and today the property is the site of the Bloomberg Tower, hosting all of the company's operations. It is also a luxury condominium, with Steve Cohen owning the penthouse and the site of the now-defunct Le Cirque. What Steve Roth thought was going to be a failure turned into a billion-dollar success for him. From a low of around five or six dollars per share, the stock today is selling at $275 per share with an enterprise value of over $2 billion, of which Vornado owns 32.4 percent. Good for him. And for me, though we failed to sell Alexander's as we had wanted, what I got, far beyond the $50,000 retainer, was a terrific example of having personally worked very hard at a deal that didn't pan out in the moment but, down the line, brought about the creation of something completely unexpected and triumphant. It really pleases me to no end to see a great outcome in a business dealing. Even though I became a kind of spectator in the Alexander's story, I truly enjoyed watching the business get to a great place.

Of course, Saks Fifth Avenue is one of the most celebrated specialty upscale department stores in New York and perhaps the United States. My experience with Saks has been interesting over the years.

I was friendly with Mel Jacobs, one of the great merchants, who was the CEO of Saks for a number of years and helped grow the company. We had discussions when he retired about working together. We met in my office on a deal one day and he asked if we could have lunch. Unfortunately, I had a lunch date already scheduled, and he understood. Eventually our meeting did take place. But sadly, Mel went home afterwards and had a heart attack that very day. I was told that I was the last person to see him. (Which reminds me to enjoy every day of your life.)

Then in 2007, I was retained by the Icelandic investment company, Baugur Group, which was then a highflyer, along with Landmark, the Dubai-based retail company, to pursue the acquisition of Saks Fifth Avenue, which was rumored to be in a position to be taken over. We had meetings with one of the largest shareholders in Mexico. The stock was selling at around fifteen dollars and my client put an indication of interest on the table at twenty-six dollars per share. They could not get financing and the board never considered the deal without any form of financing. As a result, the deal never materialized. It wasn't long before the stock dropped significantly due to a brief recession.

By 2008, Saks' stock had lost significant market value because of the recession, dropping down to a price of two dollars a share. There were rumors in the market about the potential of Saks to go into bankruptcy. I had a very good friend, Solomon Lew, the legendary retailer based in Australia who had turned around the Myer Department Store chain in Australia and then merged it into Coles Myer to become the largest retailer in Australia; he became the Chairman and CEO of Coles Myer which owned the largest supermarket chain and also the Kmart business in Australia. He wanted to acquire a business in the US and we had looked at a number of opportunities which did not develop into a deal including Kmart. Sol set his sights on taking control of Saks Fifth Avenue because he believed, due to the value of the brand name, he could make the company thrive both in the US and globally. We had several meetings and he retained Financo along with UBS to represent his company, while Saks retained Goldman Sachs. Sol's team did a substantial amount of due diligence with the team at Saks, which included Steve Sadove, who was CEO of Saks. The board clearly reviewed and was supportive of the transaction on its original offer (although they were also looking at other financing alternatives). The buyer was going to invest about $250 million as a convertible debenture, paying a small dividend but convertible into 19.9 percent of the company since if it were 20 percent or more, it would have caused the outstanding debt to come due, as the investment would be categorized as a "change in control." (Although it should be noted that Sol never set his sights on taking total control of this US asset but wanted to use his expertise in department store retailing to work with Steve whom he had a great respect for and the team at Saks to continue the growth of the business). The price to convert into common stock was around five dollars per share. However, the buyer continued to be concerned about the state of the economy and wanted additional collateral in the form of a first mortgage of the Saks flagship store on Fifth Avenue. The board turned this down and the deal died.

"I had great respect for Sol," says Steve Sadove. "He was highly accomplished and had very good perspectives on the business. He and his team went too far in looking for the additional collateral and lost out on an enormous value creating opportunity. We still talk about how it was one that he missed out on."

Subsequent to that deal, the economy improved, and the stock rose to five dollars per share. Saks went to the market and was able to raise a $300 million convert at a strike price of seven dollars a share, which was far more favorable to the company than the terms of Sol's deal. Sol lost an opportunity and the lesson learned is not to over-reach unless the seller is desperate, for nothing will happen. Do not take things for granted but always take advantage of the opportunity. There is no doubt that Sol would have worked with the Saks team to build up Saks and put it at an even greater position than it is today.

It is worth noting that both Sol and Steve attended the Financo CEO conference each year and were panelists and I have maintained a long-term relationship with them both. Some years later, I had the honor of inducting Sol into the Retail Hall of Fame at the World Retail Congress. Sol is now in the process of taking over Myer, the Australian department store chain, of which he is the largest shareholder.

That said, Richard Baker, the CEO and Governor of HBC which today owns Saks, is doing some creative things in separating the business into a retail store business and potentially spinning off the e-commerce business as Saks.com into a separate public entity.

OFF-PRICE RETAILING AND MY EXPERIENCE WITH MARSHALLS/TJMAXX

Of all my deals that did get done, the one I'm most proud of, both for its success and the vision, was representing Marshalls in a sale to TJ Maxx.

The year was 1995. Before the off-price business became a behemoth, department stores were operating well but didn't pay any attention to other sectors in the marketplace. You had many different models of retailers: the traditional department store (Macy's); the discount chain (where the growth of Walmart, Kmart, and Target were becoming more evident with the consumer shifting); the general merchandise store (including Sears, Penney's, and perhaps even Kohl's); the independent big box power players (like Home Depot and Best Buy that were growing into the strip centers); the numerous specialty stores (including American Eagle, the Limited, Abercrombie, and many others); the luxury specialty stores (like Saks, Neiman Marcus, and Barney's); the many other retailers in malls, strip centers and street locations; and the independent and growing category of e-commerce companies (Amazon). All of these were contributing to the growth of retail and the new consumer that had more and more money to spend.

What department stores did to get rid of excess merchandise was to have sales of their own, set up clearance centers, or sell to other retailers. Certainly, the most famous of these were Loehmann's and Filene's Basement, which was beneath the Filene's store in Boston. Macy's had a basement. Bloomingdale's had one of its own down in the subway. When I was working with Shoe Town, Saks 5th Avenue didn't know what to do with their leftover shoes and so they sold them to Shoe Town. (They would later create Saks Off Fifth.) So, it was more or less a conglomeration as a way to get rid of excess or dead inventory. What happened, slowly, was the off-price companies started to grow on their own. Zayre was a leading discount chain based in Boston run by Sumner Feldberg and his family. Besides the discount stores, Zayre also started what was BJs Warehouse. As the consumer switched to off-price, all of these chains began to grow and grow. Zayre brought in a guy named Bernie Cammarata. He took some of the Zayre discount stores, consolidated them, and started TJ Maxx as an off-price retailer. TJ Maxx very quickly began to pick up a lot of customers.

The same way that, over time, the department stores were consolidated and grew stronger, it was harder for the independent discounts and others to remain independent. You had Caldor, a major company in the East going bankrupt. You had Bradley's. You had Jamesway. But the department stores and all other manufacturers, especially in apparel, had always looked for ways to sell products they couldn't sell—overruns and such—and certainly, at the time, Loehmann's, which I sold twice, was one example of how a high-end retailer could grow itself. They did a phenomenal job at giving value to the customer, where you could buy things from manufacturers at a fraction of the price. So, Loehmann's was at a high-end; shopping at their stores was like a treasure hunt.

Both Marshalls (which was owned by my client, Melville Corporation) and TJ Maxx were selling medium-priced, branded labels, and they began in much the same way. They would buy up excess inventory and sell it. The bulk of their business was shoes, apparel, and home goods. All of a sudden, the business really started to grow. Marshalls, which had started up before TJ Maxx and was the model for the latter's company, had also grown significantly and was very profitable. But Marshalls started to run into problems for two reasons: one was the diversification of its parent company, Melville, which wasn't working out as well as they had hoped. They weren't paying attention to many of their businesses the way they should have, honestly. The second reason for their difficulty was that they brought in a guy who'd been the number two person at Target to run Marshalls. He decided to make Marshalls look more upscale, putting in fancier fixtures, nice tile on the floors and so on. Now, the whole premise of a Marshalls or TJ Maxx is that they try to appeal to a consumer who believes they're getting a bargain. Or, that the company actually wants to give that consumer a bargain. This was the thinking. But visually, if the stores were too fancy, the consumer would begin to pick up on the premise that the prices were too high. A very interesting way to do business, working with the ego this way. For whatever reason, after all my years doing deals with Melville, as good an operation as they were, the company was never able to turn around any of their businesses that ran into trouble. It was the same with their footwear, apparel, and accessories businesses, as well as their Linens 'n Things domestics business. Once the ship began taking on water, it was sunk, and they would either have to close or sell it. Marshalls was one of those sinking ships, and Stanley Goldstein, the CEO of Melville, asked us to find a buyer for the company.

As far as my thinking went, there were two logical choices of the other competing off-priced retailers. The first was Ross Stores. Ross primarily operated in the South, while Marshalls was, by and large, in the Northeast and the middle of the country. I went to talk to Ross, and they turned it down. My feeling was that they didn't have the guts to do an acquisition this big. Next, we went to TJX. Though we had looked at other companies, we really thought TJX was a great possibility. TJ Maxx had been built up by doing nothing less than copying the Marshalls format, so we believed some real synergies could be there between the two companies. Of course, TJX would also be interested in buying their number one competitor. All these factors played into our thinking.

I called up Sumner Feldberg and Bernie Cammarata and set up a meeting with myself and Karen Goodman, who was my "right-hand" banker. We had discussions, we signed NDAs, we exchanged information. And, lo and behold, TJX was interested.

We began to put together the deal. We had a number of meetings in both Boston and Westchester, where TJX was located, and in New York, where Melville was located, and tried to hammer out an agreement. One of the things that was holding back the right purchase price was that at the time TJ Maxx operated 551 stores and Marshalls operated about 500, and it became clear that many Marshalls stores would have to be closed because around 250 of them overlapped geographically with TJ Maxx. Meaning, you had Marshalls and TJ Maxx locations that were too close to one another, less than a few miles. Normally, what would happen with a deal like this is that the buyer would insist that the seller close those stores as part of the deal. But Melville was not willing to do this. We had to work through these differences; we did, and we negotiated a purchase price of $550 million. The deal closed on November 17, 1995. But what happened thereafter is a history lesson on how vision and insight can change the fortunes of a company. After the acquisition, TJX came to the realization that closing the overlapping stores wouldn't make sense since no more than 20 percent of the sales of the closed stores would transfer to the remaining stores. Therefore, they decided to evaluate each location, and they ended up keeping most of the stores and only closing those which were marginal or non-profitable. And even more importantly, they kept both names. The consumer had no idea that both stores were owned by the same party. The financial world knew it, but not the consumer. To this day, although Marshalls and TJ Maxx have done some combined-advertising, most consumers still don't know that the stores are owned by one company. Brilliantly, TJX also combined the back-of-the-house of these two stores into what became Marmax. The merchant team, financial team, and the IT team, all came to work the same backend of the business. The result of that decision was colossal. TJX's net income at the time of the closing was $83 million. Two years later, it grew to $365 million. The market capitalization went from $1.1 billion in 1995 to $3 billion the next year and then to $5.7 billion, then $7.5 billion and onward. By 2004 it was $11.7 billion. Today, the company has revenue of $40.6 billion, an EBITDA (Earnings Before Interest, Taxes and Depreciation and Amortization) of $5.1 billion, and a market capitation of $75.4 billion with another $10 billion in cash for an enterprise value of $84.8 billion. It sells for an EBITDA multiple of 16.4 times. In March of 2021, TJX announced that they would open eighty-one new stores in the US. This is twenty-five years after the deal, and they're still growing and growing. Need I say anything more?

Well, yes. I'll say that the success of the Marshalls/TJX deal starts with the fact that I was working with a group at TJX that saw its future and were running towards it. Sure, at the time, no one knew that the result would be quite so meteoric. And indeed, there's always some luck involved. The rise and fall of the economy, for instance—you can't control *that*. But the TJX people had such a deep understanding of where the industry was heading and, because of this, we all benefited and continue to, all the way to this day. You can't imagine the happiness that this deal brings me on a regular basis. After so many years, I see TJX continuing to thrive, and it fills me up with so much good feeling. It means I brought the right parties together and that we did the right thing, and to me, that is everything. In my mind, of all the thousands of deals I have done, this was *the* most successful and personally rewarding opportunity for creating real value for the surviving corporation.

Financo CEO Dinner in 2005—Bottom row from left to right: Gilbert Harrison, Kip Tindell (founder and Chairman of The Container Store); from top left: Lew Frankfort (Chairman and CEO of Coach, Inc), Burt Tansky (Chairman and CEO of Neiman Marcus), Mackey McDonald (Chairman and CEO of VF Corporation), and Len Schlesinger (Vice Chairman and COO of Limited Brands).

CHAPTER 4

The Event of the Year:
The Financo CEO Forum and Dinner

"IT WAS EVERYTHING SHORT OF fisticuffs at the Financo Forum Monday night as senior retail executives testily debated price, the Internet, and expansion—all while trying to outshine each other," said *Women's Wear Daily* on January 13th, 2010. "The Financo event, always a lively affair, this time featured the outspoken Sir Philip Green, Topshop's owner, whose repartee swung from the jovial in nature to downright confrontational...The other panelists were Millard "Mickey" Drexler, chairman and CEO of J.Crew Group, who added an edge by debating the importance of price with Bruce Rockowitz, president of Li & Fung Ltd., and was needling Rockowitz into disclosing his retail clients, but Rockowitz resisted. James Fielding, president of Disney Stores, and Solomon Lew, chairman of Australia-based The Just group, rounded out the panel."

What a scene. What a fracas. What a good time. Oh, how far our annual CEO dinners had come.

In the early-1980s, the National Retail Federation Convention in January was probably the highlight of all the retail conferences in the country. It was a four-day period in New York in which basically every important retail CEO from the United States and many from Europe and Asia would attend meetings. As you might imagine, with everyone in New York at the same conference, it was an important time for getting new business and information.

I had a friend, Ken Walker, who was probably the foremost expert in architectural design for department and specialty stores. During a NRF around 1980, Ken and I were discussing some business, and he told me that he was hosting a small dinner at the Four Seasons Hotel where several of the leading CEOs would be getting together. He asked me if I would like to attend and I said, of course, that I would be there.

"I was always looking for top retailers who were focused on new design ideas," says Ken Walker, when asked about why he hosted the first dinner.

And at that evening's dinner, he certainly *had* that: Gordon Segal of Crate & Barrel, Don Fisher of the Gap, Andre Meyer from Galeries Lafayette in Paris, among others. And what a night the lot of us had. It's not often you get to sit around a table with so many brilliant retailers on a private, confidential level and reflect on the past year as well as the one to come. But it was also a more casual get-together, one where we could talk to one another in a manner that was more open than you'd be able to at, say, a board room on the top floor of an office tower. It was a way to get a little more personal and deepen our relationships.

I found the dinner to be such a pleasure that when the NRF came around the following year, I called up Ken and said that we should do it again. He agreed. Gordon and Don and Andre did too—and we were back at the Four Seasons Hotel, having yet another great time. A year had passed and a lot of business had gotten done, and we discussed it all, again in this more relaxed setting that allowed us to really open up and have a good time. By the end of the dinner, I was in awe of what a special night we had put together, now for the second year in a row. It was just one of those things—the magic was there in the room, and you were thrilled to be a part of it.

As you might have already gathered, I'm someone who likes to push his luck. Moreover, I don't believe that you can ever have too much of a good thing. And so, we did the dinner a third and fourth time during those next NRF conferences. We might have one new face on this occasion and another new one at the next, but you always had the core group of Ken and Gordon and Don and Andre and myself, and you always had the excitement of being back together once again and the camaraderie and the pleasure.

These dinners became the stuff of legend.

In fact, when I sold Financo to Lehman Brothers in 1985, part of what Lehman was intrigued with *was* the CEO dinner. They wanted me to bring it into the company and make it bigger. So we did, doing a night with American Express and Lehman Brothers that Jim Robinson, the chief executive of American Express, would host, and we turned it into a very good affair. But it had grown into something different with Lehman. It was still effective as far as discussing and doing business, but it was less intimate, less personal.

When I got Financo back from Lehman in 1989, I decided to continue the dinner under my own auspices. At the time, Goldman Sachs had a major dinner during the NRF on the Tuesday of that week and Deloitte Touche had something on Sunday night. We got the Monday night slot.

Over the years, we grew the dinner, and it really started to become something. We hosted our event at the Harmonie Club on East 60th Street between 5th Avenue and Madison where I was a member. The first couple of years, we would only use the first floor. A decade later, we had to rent out three. We'd begin the evening with a presentation followed by cocktails and then a smaller, select dinner.

I would meet over the weekend beforehand with the Financo bankers and then, at the dinner, I would put a banker between two people who we thought could do a deal together. Or, if they were already clients, we would put them next to each other without a banker. Either way, every table had two bankers at it.

Initially, we limited the dinner to CEOs, COOs, and some of the acquisition people who we were close to, but very few private equity people and professional people. The problem with the professional people, even those who I considered to be wonderful individuals, was that they would spend the time trying to solicit clients. And as much as I went to other events, I knew how to solicit clients tactfully while in those environments. (Though, I'll share a few words on a stickier conference moment later in the book). But a lot of people do not have that tact. At the dinner, we had no other investment bankers. But you couldn't believe the balls certain people had, asking to be invited. There were CEOs who used other banking firms to do their business, and they would call up, looking for a spot. We would always tell them that there was no room.

At the dinner, there was no press, and everything was totally off-the-record. I would go around and ask the executives how the holiday sales had gone and what they were doing now and what their projections were for the year to come. And while there's no such thing as a free lunch, we never charged anyone to attend. But, if we picked up one or two deals as a result of the dinner, the night would have more than paid for itself.

Stacy Berns, my dear friend, who heads Berns Communications Group (of which I was the first client), was totally instrumental. I would make the phone calls and land the speakers. Stacy would do the press. In the early years we didn't have sponsors because we didn't want to be beholden to anybody. But as the dinner grew and became more costly, we decided to do so, and Stacy brought in MasterCard as a sponsor. This turned out to be very good. You have to remember, the event was in January, so it was right after the holidays but before a lot of companies had reported their earnings.

"But that's what made it so interesting," said Berns, "because if you go to an investor conference, you see a number of CEOs of publicly traded companies that are given pre-approved presentations that don't give any information at all. We had people that felt like they could speak openly and at some point, it would become a dialogue with the audience. So, for instance, Mickey Drexler, who attended most of the

Financo dinners, would ask very controversial questions to panelists, and it became this open forum. That was very different from a presentation that's prepared where no one's really saying anything. It got to the point where the press was calling it the must-have invite."

"I'll never forget that dinner," says retail icon, Mickey Drexler. "I've always been allergic to panels, and that dinner reinforced my allergy. But I must say, I had a great time there arguing with a number of panelists. For me, I found it stimulating and fun. I'm not sure my panelists felt the same way."

As for the panelists, we always tried to put people together that would create interesting synergy. For instance, in 2014, I had Tommy Hilfiger, Aerin Lauder, Andrew Rosen, and Marigay McKee. They all knew each other. The back and forth that you would get because they were friends was very interesting. We would also look for retail or apparel executives who were doing something particular within the year, which is very important. But the list of people was astonishing.

"The first year I was there, in 2006, it was Jeff Bezos and P Diddy, for instance," said Berns. "Which was so indicative of how the retail sector was about to change and how Gilbert was at the forefront of that change. I don't know anyone who's gotten Jeff Bezos to speak at an industry event. He always says no. But Bezos thought that if he were going to speak at one place, in front of all the retail leaders, then it would be this event."

Over the years, we had almost every major retailer in the country on the panel, as well as many from outside the United States. Allow me a moment here to make your eyes grow wide with disbelief with the full year-by-year list of panelists from 2004 through 2016. It's astonishing:

2004

Lee Capps III, President Operating Services, Kellwood Company

Paul Charron, former Chairman and CEO, Liz Claiborne Inc.

William Fung, Managing Director, Li & Fung Ltd.
Ira Kalish, Global Director, Deloitte Research
Mackey McDonald, Chairman and CEO, VF Corporation

2005

Lew Frankfort, Chairman and CEO, Coach, Inc.
Mackey McDonald, Chairman and CEO, VF Corporation
Leonard Schlesinger, former Vice Chairman and COO,
Limited Brands, current President of Babson College
Burt Tansky, President and CEO, Neiman
Marcus Group Ltd LLC
Kip Tindell, President and CEO, The Container Store Group, Inc.

2006

Jeffrey Bezos, founder & CEO, Amazon.com, Inc.
Sean Combs, Chairman, Sean Jean Clothing, Inc.
Michael Gould, Chairman and CEO, Bloomingdale's
Mindy Grossman, former Head of Global Apparel,
Nike, Inc., current CEO of IAC/InterActiveCorp
Heinz Krogner, Group CEO, Esprit Holdings Ltd.

2007

Bernd Beetz, CEO, Coty Inc.
Giovanna Furlanetto, Chairman, Furla SPA
George Jones, CEO and President, Borders Group, Inc.
Matt Rubel, CEO and President, Collective Brands, Inc.
Steve Sadove, CEO, Saks, Inc.
Trudy Sullivan, former President, Liz Claiborne,
Inc., current President and CEO, Talbots, Inc.

2008

Bonnie Brooks, former President, Lane Crawford Joyce
Group, current President and CEO, Hudson's Bay Company
Jim Gold, Chief Executive, Bergdorf Goodman Inc.

Robert Hanson, President, Levi's Strauss & Co.

Jon Asgeir Johannesson, Executive Chairman, Baugur Group

Mike Ullman, Chairman and CEO, J.C. Penney Company, Inc.

2009

Mickey Drexler, Chairman and CEO, J.Crew Group, Inc.

Mindy Grossman, CEO, HSNi, LLC

Gordon Segal, founder and Chairman, Crate & Barrel

David Simon, Chairman and CEO, Simon Property Group, Inc.

Burt Tansky, Chairman and CEO, Neiman
Marcus Group Ltd LLC

2010

Mickey Drexler, Chairman and CEO, J.Crew Group, Inc.

James Fielding, President, Disney Store

Sir Philip Green, owner, Arcadia Group
of Brands including Top Shop

Solomon Lew, Chairman, The Just Group

Betsey McLaughlin, CEO, Hot Topic, Inc.

Bruce Rockowitz, President, Li & Fung, (Trading) Ltd.

2011

Tom Arrix, Vice President, US Sales, Facebook, Inc.

Ben Fischman, CEO, Rue La La

Daniel Schock, Retail Industry Director, Google LLC

Chip Wilson, founder, Chairman of the Board and Chief
Innovation and Branding Officer, Lululemon Athletica

Nicole Lapin, anchor, Worldwide Exchange, CNBC (Moderator)

2012

Chris Burch, founder and CEO, C. Wonder

Susan Lyne, Chairman, Gilt Groupe, LP

Kevin Plank, Founder and CEO, Under Armour, Inc.

Walter Robb, Co-CEO, Whole Foods Market, Inc.

Margaret Brennan, anchor, Bloomberg TV, (moderator)

2013

Paul Blum, CEO, Juicy Couture, Inc.

Lew Frankfort, Chairman and CEO, Coach,
Inc. (currently Tapestry, Inc.)

Danny Meyer, founder and CEO, Union
Square Hospitality Group

Eric Wiseman, Chairman, President and CEO, VF Corporation

Sagra Maceira de Rosen, Strategy and
Investment Advisor (Moderator)

2014

Tommy Hilfiger, founder, Tommy Hilfiger U.S.A, Inc.

Aerin Lauder, founder and Creative Director, Aerin, Inc.

Andrew Rosen, founder and CEO, Theory

Marigay McKee, President, Saks, Inc. (moderator)

2015

Diane Von Furstenberg, Fashion Designer

2016

Drew Barrymore, Actor

"One of my winter highlights when I was CEO of Manhattan Industries, was the annual Financo dinner organized and conducted by Gilbert Harrison," says Laurence Leeds. "The dinner, which always occurred during the second week of January, was an industry 'must-attend.' This gathering of industry-leading figures almost always developed into a formidable exchange of ideas, so much that CEOs would arrange their schedules to assure to be able to attend the event. Prominent members of the press were always on hand to cover the event, and news headlines frequently occurred derived from the evening's discussion. Gilbert Harrison was the stalwart MC and spent much of the evening calling on various CEOs to tell the group about the latest events and trends in the marketplace."

"The Financo dinners at the Harmonie Club were the most original and enjoyable annual events each year," says Martin Miller, a longtime client and friend of mine, who has spent his entire life in the apparel business. "Always during the January market week, it allowed me to see and visit more important members of our industry than I could have possibly met up with individually. The panels were original and very informative, but most important, they were filled with attendees who had specific and worthwhile backgrounds and opinions. All the executives and princip[a]ls and guests were important people I looked forward to seeing. I'm still friends with many of my dinner companions from the Financo CEO Dinners. I remember offering Gilbert a commission on a customer who I met at one of them. The event was the highlight of every January market week."

Indeed they were.

Perhaps one thing that I didn't do at our events was have enough of the younger, newer executives speaking. Maybe because I'm an old-timer and I knew old-timers. Sure, Aerin Lauder and Marigay McKee were young, but we didn't pull in as many of the up-and-coming entrepreneurs that maybe we should have as they were building their businesses. And while it was an extremely successful affair, that's one of the things that I wish I'd done differently.

But when I think back on how I was able to establish the name Financo as a financial advisory firm, perhaps the thing I did to differentiate us most could be seen in our ability to build up our reputation—and to that end, the Financo Dinner was absolutely critical. If no one knew who we were, how would we get business? Certainly, one way we did that was through word-of-mouth from a happy client or their lawyer, an accountant, or other advisor. And the press had also been very good to us. I had no hesitation in talking to journalists both on the record and off. I know many people are afraid of the press and are concerned that they'll misinterpret what's said. Luckily, I never had that problem, even with the people at *Forbes* magazine, who in those days were difficult to deal with.

Looking back, I realize that conferences were essential to building our reputation and bringing in business since we were still the "little independent guy." I tried to attend as many industry conferences as possible. This not only helped with my image but also in developing relationships with clients. Initially, I was invited to conferences sponsored by some of the bulge bracket investment firms, but as I grew Financo they came to view me as the competition. One example of this was a Merrill Lynch conference where I sat next to Raymond Zimmerman, the founder and CEO of Service Merchandise. This led to not only a long-term friendship but also substantial business. However, when the bankers at Merrill saw this, I was never again invited to their conferences. The same was true with Goldman Sachs. When one of my clients was talking at their conferences, they would give me a one-way pass to listen to their presentation, but I was then expected to leave.

At another conference before I was "banned," I was standing with a group of people, talking. Among them was Marvin Traub, Allen Questrom, and Donald Trump, who, at the time, controlled Alexander's. Marvin, Allen, and I all had our badges on, but Donald did not. Another person joined the group that none of us really knew. He looked around, saw our name-badges, and said hello to the three of us. When he came to Donald, he said, "I am so-and-so. What's your name?" Donald could not believe that *he* was not known to this person. It must have been a blow to his ego, as he took the badge out of his pocket and kept it on for the rest of the event. So, as you can see, it wasn't all business. We had some good laughs as well.

It was amazing what you would learn at these conferences. Especially important in that regard was the "Retail CEO Roundtable."

"The original event was held at FIT in Fall 2009," says Eric Hertz, president of the Center for Retail Real Estate. "FIT had planned a major industry conference that year featuring a panel of leading retail CEOs chaired by Terry Lundgren. Since I was the Chairman of FIT,

I was very involved. However, due to the deep and sudden impact of the Great Recession, none of the participants (including Terry) were willing to go ahead with a large public event. So, we decided to hold a 'closed' session of not more than twenty-five retail CEOs where Terry and the other attendees could discuss the industry's problems in confidence, and attempt to come up with solutions and strategies.

"Robin Lewis launched the discussion with a provocative state-of-the-industry presentation. The event was so successful that we decided to keep the dialogue going twice a year, always in a 'private and confidential' environment. When I left FIT in the spring of 2010 to pursue my own consulting business, Gilbert invited me to continue co-chairing the event with him, and we held them in participating execs' boardrooms, and it continued (with only a few interruptions) until 2017.

"It's fair to say that out of this nine-year-long tradition many innovative retail strategies were hatched, and a great deal of camaraderie was generated among the retail industry's leadership. And it was a great personal and professional pleasure collaborating with Gilbert over all of those years."

The sessions were hosted at Bloomingdale's, Barney's, Bergdorf's, Saks, and other retail headquarters in New York.

At the last of these sessions, in May of 2017, Lord & Taylor hosted, and it was quite the group of CEOs who gathered to speak, including Claudio Del Vecchio, Chairman and CEO of Brooks Brothers; William Taubman of Taubman Centers; Marc Metrick, President of Saks Fifth Avenue; Marigay McKee, President of MM Luxe Consulting; Robin Lewis, CEO of the Robin Report; Ken Himmel, President and CEO of Related Urban and, of course, Mickey Drexler; and many others. Burt Tansky, the CEO of Neiman Marcus, co-hosted with me. Everyone there addressed some of the most critical questions of the time, such as these, taken straight from the record of the event:

"Given the current turbulent climate for retail, how do you see the balance of 2017 unfolding for retailers? Which companies appear most likely to survive and grow? Which will experience the greatest challenges? How can e-commerce be effectively leveraged to support in-store performance? How are "click and collect" strategies performing? What has been the impact on merchandise returns and/or add-on purchases? How will consumer spending continue to play out across the retail channels—luxury, mid-tier, and mass—this year and next? What can retailers do to continue to stimulate renewed consumer interest in shopping and a willingness to spend? How are shopping centers evolving to enhance the customer experience? Are there additional opportunities for collaboration between mall owners and retailers to help drive consumer engagement and purchasing? As consumers continue to be more price sensitive, do you envision a continuation of the outsized growth rate of the off-price sector? Are we in danger of oversaturating the marketplace for off-price and outlet-based retail? What is the near-term outlook for the luxury sector? How do you expect luxury and designer merchandise to perform during the balance of 2017? Do you anticipate a continued downsizing of retail space through 2017? Will major retailers continue to close underperforming doors and downsize store models during the months ahead? How can physical retailers market themselves most effectively to millennials? What types of messaging are most effective, and how can brick-and-mortar retailers compete successfully with e-commerce players? How can retailers provide a greater sense of fashion urgency? What role will technology play in this initiative? Which product categories are currently your best performers? Which are underperforming? Where will consumers accelerate their spending, and where do you see them holding back? How can traditional retailers effectively compete with fast fashion resources such as H&M and Zara? Are efforts underway to accelerate turn and thereby create an ongoing sense of newness? How can retailers create a more compelling shopping experience? Which companies are successfully forging new ground in customer engagement? What is the outlook for credit availability through 2017? Do you expect a gradual increase in interest rates to unfold into 2018? How have languishing middle class income levels affected the availability of consumer credit for mainstream retailers? Have ongoing low fuel prices and interest rates resulted in a greater consumer willingness to spend?"

You would come away from these sessions, which for the most part were totally confidential and off the record, with such a great perspective on what lay ahead directly from your peers. After all, you had just heard some of the most knowledgeable people in the field address nearly all the major questions a retailer could fathom. It was breathtaking, to say the least.

I acted as a moderator or a panelist at the World Retail Congress and the Financial Times Luxury Conference, both of which were held annually throughout the world. I met so many people in these conferences, which certainly benefited our business but also allowed a lot of travel to see different cities, from London, Paris, Venice, Rome, Tokyo, San Francisco, Las Vegas, Washington DC, Miami, and Palm Beach. Additionally, I participated in ShopTalk Las Vegas, ShopTalk Europe, Business Summit "Retail Business Russia," the YPO and the ABA's annual conference, the WWD (Women's Wear) and FW (Footwear News), and Beauty conferences through the year including their annual.

But remember, back in the early 2000s, there weren't many independent investment banking firms. Financo was really the first boutique investment firm specializing in retail, merchandise, and other consumer-related business. In time, some of the big names on Wall

Street would leave their respective firms to start their own compa-nies, but that hadn't happened yet. What we did more than anything to expand and get new clients and differentiate ourselves from the large firms like Goldman Sachs, Morgan Stanley, and Bear Stearns really *was* the Financo Annual CEO dinner. It became the cornerstone of increasing our brand awareness. The press loved to cover it, and it brought in many new clients. Those who attended loved it too. But more than anyone, I loved it. The occasion brought me tremendous joy. Seeing everyone from the industry come together at the Harmonie Club provided a yearly reminder of just how many great relationships I had developed and of how fortunate I had been in my work.

Gilbert with his parents at his graduation from Wharton in 1962.

| CHAPTER 5 |

Great Learning Moments: Valuable Lessons from Business That I Wish to Pass Down

I'VE LONG HAD A GREAT history at the Wharton School at the University of Pennsylvania. I received my BS in Economics from the Wharton School in 1962 and my LLD from the School of Law in 1965. But not only did I attend as a student, my wife, children, and now my grandchildren, went to either Wharton or the College at the University of Pennsylvania. I also served for over fifteen years on the Board of the Wharton School, and Shelley and I have made many contributions over the years, including a professorship at Wharton, a study hall at Wharton, as well as a portion of the funds needed for Ben on the Bench, the historical campus landmark dedicated by my class of 1962. Moreover, Shelley and I were founders of the Penn Club of New York. In many senses, Wharton and Penn feel like another home to me.

Back in the 1970s, in the early years of Financo when I was in Philadelphia, I had the wonderful privilege of teaching a mergers course there called Management 49. Passing on knowledge to those students coming up—what a crucial experience. A beautiful one, really. My class was limited to twelve to fifteen students, and we met once a week for two and a half hours. Many of my own students from the Management 49 course have gone on to have great Wall Street and business careers. I still see some of them. They'll pop up on the other side of the table during a meeting or at a conference or perhaps in a restaurant, and many of them—one of whom is a client today—still call me Professor. I take pride in that.

It's now been more than forty years since I taught that course at Wharton, and as you might imagine, my knowledge of the field has deepened. But if I were back in that classroom standing before my beloved students, I would insist that they open their ears and take in these few critical lessons I learned along the way, all of which remain vital to me.

TEAMWORK

If anything came out of the four years that I spent at Lehman, it was realizing how teamwork is essential to being successful. At Lehman, between the politics and the bureaucracy, no one seemed to care about anyone but themselves. As previously noted, bankers didn't want to share deals with anyone because they feared they would get a smaller bonus. Unbelievable. When I restarted Financo in 1989, I told all of my bankers that in addition to their base salaries, their bonuses would be determined according to three principals: the overall profit of the firm, the individual's performance, and teamwork. Financo bankers could be substantially penalized by not working together. I also didn't do what other firms did—pay bankers a percentage of the fees they generated. In my opinion, this practice discourages teamwork. Everyone I employed at Financo seemed to understand this. Instead, at the end of each year, I would meet with my President and CFO and go through every deal to understand what the firm and each individual banker had done and how everyone worked together. From there, I would determine the size of a bonus. I'm proud that Financo practiced this philosophy, and I have little doubt that the benefits were innumerable and central to our success. People thought of me as not only their employer but as a "benevolent dictator," because I controlled the purse strings but also tried to be fair and generous, and that's how I liked it.

CONFIDENTIALITY

Whether practicing law, acting as a financial advisor, investment banker, or a consultant, confidentiality is critical in this business. Should there be any leak of discussions, a deal may be undermined. Of much graver concern, there may be significant liability and even SEC violations.

The need to keep things confidential first dawned on me when practicing law in New York at Mermelstein. One day, a client of ours was in the bathroom at the Plaza Hotel, and two people unknown to him came in and started talking about seeing the CEO of a certain company and how they intended to make an offer to buy a division of it. They actually said the price they were willing to pay, right there in the bathroom of the Plaza Hotel, where, for good reason, they thought they could speak without fear of consequences. Well, the client overheard them, wanted to buy the business, called up the same CEO, and made a higher offer than what the bathroom-talkers were willing to pay. Next thing you know, he'd won the business. It was very successful, and he made millions on the acquisition. When I heard this story the first time, I couldn't believe it. What were the chances something like this could happen? Almost zero. And yet it *had* happened, and for the bathroom-talkers the results were catastrophic.

When starting at Blank Rome, we were told never to discuss confidential information on an elevator, in a train, on the subway, at any public gatherings, or any place where someone might hear the discussion. Ed Rome even showed the attorneys a video on the importance of confidentiality. It seemed silly at the time: A man named Bob was riding on the Metroliner from New York. Sitting on a nearby seat were two lawyers discussing their strategy on how they were going to win a lawsuit against Ed in court later that day. Bob, it turned out, was Ed's client—and Bob got off that Metroliner and went immediately to Ed and told him the strategy and, of course, Ed won the lawsuit.

When you're young and you see a film like that, you imagine it's a waste of time. But you've got to take it seriously. If you don't, you could very well pay a price, and if you do, the price is most likely going to be so substantial that you'll be kicking yourself because of it for the rest of your life.

So yes, at Blank Rome, the importance of confidentiality was ingrained in me, and it was something that I was very careful about. I loved to tell stories about what was happening in the industry, especially with colleagues, but I would never discuss anything that I was in the process of working on (including many of the insights in this book which have never been previously discussed, but all these years later, no longer pose any confidentiality problems).

Another instance having to do with confidentiality—one I did not find out about until years after the fact—concerned my representation of Hasbro in its purchase of Milton Bradley. I had to go to Providence to meet with the CEO and others at Hasbro on a regular basis and, knowing that I had young children, the company would always send me off with some of the latest toys as gifts to bring home for them. Well, my daughter, Nancy, was on the school bus, sitting with one of her friends one day, and she told that very friend that her father had just come back from Hasbro and was working on something great. While she didn't know what it was, the other girl happened to tell her father about my dealings, and the father got the idea in his head to buy Hasbro stock. He told me this many years later but claimed that he never, in fact, bought the stock. A good thing, too, for it could have been a disaster. Information, in the wrong hands can lead to great and unknown consequences. In this case, that information was in the hands of a child who was advising her father on his stock purchases based on my daughter's inside information. The SEC might have had a field day with that one.

Speaking of the SEC, here's another deal that raises important issues around confidentiality:

I was working with Interco on its acquisition of Queen Casuals, a Philadelphia-based apparel company. The CEO of Interco called the CEO of Devon Apparel, which was already owned by Interco. The purpose of the call was to tell the Devon CEO (on a confidential basis) that the acquisition of another apparel company (Queen Casuals) would be announced the next day. Sitting in the CEO's office was another person who overheard the conversation. The deal was done, and a few months later, the SEC subpoenaed our firm. They had started an investigation into insider trading, and they were going after a lot of people in Philadelphia who knew about the deal. Since we were the investment bankers, we certainly were a potential target. But we knew nothing about these purchases, and everyone in our firm had signed a confidentiality agreement. Nevertheless, we had to retain lawyers to represent us. The cost to our firm was substantial, and in the end, the SEC found out that the person in Devon's office that day was the buyer. He was fined and, I believe, sentenced to time in prison. The lesson being: you never know. In this instance, someone overheard a piece of sensitive information, got a funny idea in his head, and then we *all* had to pay a price.

In a similar situation, we were retained to find a purchaser to buy Sam Goody. Best Buy had made an offer to the company, but the majority owner wanted us to find another firm at a higher price. We were paid a retainer and went to work. Because there was a recession going on and because record stores were losing their audience, we were not successful and Best Buy did indeed acquire the firm. A month or so later, the SEC issued us a subpoena, and we had to retain lawyers which were very costly. It turned out that this majority owner, who was getting over $100 million for his stock, had gone out the day before the deal was announced to buy shares of Best Buy for his children. Can you imagine that! Just incredible. Anyway, on several occasions we, along with our attorneys from Skadden Arps, had to go meet with the SEC who had opened an investigation into the situation. In the middle of it all, however, September 11 happened. At the time, the SEC's office in New York was located in the World Trade Center. All their records were lost in the destruction. In those days, we didn't have the cloud, and the SEC did very little backing up of files. As it turned out, the lawyer working for the SEC happened to have backed up the files on his home computer, and eventually the majority owner of Sam Goody was convicted. But why would someone getting over $100 million try to make another few million? It's unconscionable. Bulls win, bears win, and pigs go to the slaughter. We were very lucky because we had an indemnification agreement with the company and were able to recoup over $200,000 in legal fees. But of course, we lost many hours of work because of the situation, and remember—as a service organization, time is money.

GOOD HIRING PRACTICES/MAINTAINING A HAPPY OFFICE

Having strong relationships with the people at my firm, those who I saw every day, was something we worked hard to achieve. My belief has always been that one bad apple spoils the bunch. When I interviewed potential bankers, I also tried to meet their spouses or significant others, especially those of our managing directors, who were the top people working with us. Many of our bankers were just out of college or had worked at other firms, but we would do everything we could to get to know them. We mostly interviewed at the Wharton School but also at NYU, Columbia University, and the University of Michigan. Along with one or two of my colleagues, I would go to the campuses, and in addition to the one-to-one interview, we would take a small group to dinner. As we narrowed the field, we would invite a group of prospective hires to our office for what we called Super Sunday and spend the day with all the bankers—from the top people to the analysts speaking with them. Many of our younger people were the very best at helping us decide who to hire. Many had gone to the same schools, were in the same fraternities and, though still starting out, brought a special strength, ability, and insight into our search. Additionally, the group we hired as summer interns allowed us to see the production and work ethic of a potential long-term Financo person, and we usually took on all but one or two to become full-time analysts when they graduated from their respective colleges. Every year we would have a holiday party at either my home or another venue and spouses and significant others were invited as well. Once a year, we also had an outing at my home in Southampton. It would start on a Thursday for only the top people, and we would have a total strategy meeting and dinner. The next day, the rest of the firm would come out, including the entire support staff, for a day of fun. This was very successful. For the company to operate well, we needed to create an environment that was hospitable to those who made it what it was day in, day out, and to do that, it is important to spend social time out of the office as a firm. Everything we did was designed to try to make the workplace an environment that people wanted to be at and where they felt they belonged—that we weren't just another *big shop* like some of the other investment firms.

MIXING PRIVATE EQUITY AND INVESTMENT BANKING

Over the years, I have flirted with private equity.

When Financo first came along, my partner, Steve Klein, resisted any involvement with private equity. He had his reasons, namely that he preferred to focus his attention on real estate, where we had already invested quite profitably. But after we broke up, I formed Financo Investors Fund with Victor Barnett and Arnold Hoffman. We basically broke even with the ten investments, which was unfortunate. Had we been successful, think of what might have been.

Around 1993, we started Mercantile Capital Partners along with my son, Ed, who served as one of the MDs, in addition to some of the people from Financo. Two deals that really paid off for us with over 30 percent Internal Rate of Return were Stuart Weitzman and Tommy Bahama, as they were both companies for which we had the sell-side, and we were able to get a participation in the equity of the new company. Both deals had an excellent rate of return. The other deals did adequately or failed because we didn't have the right amount of capital and the outside manager we hired did not do a good job. In both cases, there was, in my opinion, an inherent conflict between my acting as a financial advisor and doing private equity, though. I was wedded to being a financial advisor and never spent the energy on the private equity side to lead it forward. You can only wear so many caps. But, looking at the success of many of the private equity firms, perhaps we lost a real opportunity.

CHEMISTRY

When a company is being bought or sold, you have to make sure the chemistry is right. It's very important in these deals. In most cases, the founders of entrepreneurial companies when bought up by bigger companies are meant to stay. But if you put millions of dollars into a founder's pocket and you don't treat them correctly, they'll walk. And, if you're keeping a founder and giving that founder millions of dollars, you also have to find ways to keep that person incentivized. Sometimes the founders will tell you, "I'm willing to stay for three years and make a transition." If that happens, the key thing you have to do is make sure you can promote someone at the company into the CEO position or go out and hire a new CEO. That is critical in the dynamic for making a successful acquisition.

But as far as chemistry, there can be other factors. As an example, I had done a lot of work for the largest retail specialty store in Canada, Dylex, when it bought Brooks Fashion Store. But an executive at

Dylex had broken away from the company and founded a Canadian chain called Le Senza, which was dominant in Canada the same way Victoria's Secret was dominant in the US. They also had licenses all over the world. So, I was retained by Les Wexner to try and acquire this company. We ended up buying it, and for the first time Les—who for reasons that I never before understood, as previously discussed—expanded beyond the continental US. He seemed pleased that he was going global. But he made one crucial mistake, and it undermined the whole deal: the president of La Senza demanded that its headquarters remain in Canada, separate from Victoria's Secret offices in the US. So, there was never a *true* merger, nor the synergies to take advantage of the combination. It became a sour point between Les and myself, and La Senza was given away for next to nothing in 2019.

SHOWING UP

As with anything in life, you've got to be there. And if you're not *there*, then you're not going to get very far. Sometimes we have to learn this the hard way.

I had gotten to know the Pentland Group, the British shoe retailer who had invested somewhere around $75,000 into Reebok in the infancy of the company and became the second largest shareholder after the founder. (Talk about timing, Pentland Group eventually took out over $700 million on the company.) Stephen Rubin OBE, the chairman and CEO of Pentland, and I worked on a number of deals, including Speedo when they acquired it. Meanwhile, we were looking at other companies that might be a good fit. Converse was on our radar. The company had gone bankrupt, but the feeling was that it had great potential. So, I went with Rubin's CFO to attend the bankruptcy auction, and we tried to buy Converse. Unfortunately, Rubin couldn't come with us. He would have had to fly from London to New York. Ordinarily that wouldn't have been an issue, but he was sick with a terrible cold. Our authority to bid was limited to a certain number, and the auction was going down to the wire. Though we were right there, people began to outbid us. I tried to get Rubin on the phone in London to get permission to up our number. I called him again and again, but he wouldn't pick up. Again, he was ill, and with the time difference, he was very likely asleep. In the end, we only needed about $1 million more than we were authorized to spend, but without Rubin's go-ahead, we couldn't do it. And so, Pentland was *not* the next owner of Converse. It was enormously frustrating. In 2019, Converse had almost $2 billion in sales. So *please*, do remember the importance of showing up. And, if you absolutely cannot, in instances such as these, do make sure to deputize someone with the proper authority to make a crucial decision at the critical time.

DO NOT UNDERESTIMATE ANYONE

In 1968, the world was crazy with mergers and acquisitions as well as initial public offering known as IPOs. I was in Philadelphia with my wife Shelley and our young son, Edward, working at Blank Rome. (Robin and Nancy had not yet been born.) One of my first assignments at Blank Rome was to work with one of the firm's partners on taking Levitz Furniture public. In those days, Levitz was one of the "hottest" stocks in the country. The closing took place at the New York offices of Bache & Company, then one of the leading Wall Street firms. It was one of the first occasions that I had attended this type of closing. Ralph Levitz, the Chairman and CEO of Levitz Furniture, received two checks from the public offering—one was for the company in the amount of about $10 million, and the other was for the sale of his own stock which totaled around $6 million, huge amounts of money at that time. After the closing, we all went to lunch at Delmonico's, in its day one of the most famous Wall Street eating establishments. While the bankers and lawyers were well-dressed, Ralph Levitz and others from his company, while now very wealthy, were not especially done up for the luncheon and didn't come off as especially "sophisticated." Well, the waiters were treating Ralph very unpleasantly. We suffered through lunch, and when Ralph was finally presented with these two checks, he said that he was going to get even with the waiter.

At the time, people didn't use credit cards the way they do today, and while Ralph probably had a lot of cash in his pocket, when presented with the bill, he took the $10 million check out, gave it to the waiter and said with a straight face, "Can you please give me the change?"

The waiter, also with a straight face, said, "Sir, do you have anything smaller?"

At which point, Ralph gave him the $6 million check and finally got a smile from the waiter.

Which is to say: in business, as in life, do not *ever* underestimate anyone.

WHY DON'T THEY LISTEN

While at Lehman, I did work for Sears, which at the time was still a strong company but was quickly losing its luster. They asked me to set up a meeting with the Chairman of IKEA, which I did. Their office was in Denmark. We flew to Copenhagen and had a great meeting, and Ingvar Kamprad, the owner of IKEA, was most impressed and suggested that Sears find one or two sites next to a Sears location. They would build an Ikea store there and should it work, then he would consider merging into Sears. I called him a year later, and this is what he told me: Sears had never come up with a site.

I was shocked. They hadn't come up with a site? Was it possible? Indeed it was.

And look at the potential of a merger with Home Depot. When HD's stock value was around $400 billion, Bernie Marcus, the Founder and CEO of Home Depot (one of the smartest people I knew and who had built a great company), was not sure how he would get to the next step and was open to merging with a strategic partner for around $700 billion. I thought of Sears because their home department was very good, and the combination could be terrific. Unfortunately, Sears also passed on Home Depot.

Next for Home Depot, we thought of Kmart.

At the time, Kmart owned Builders Square, the San Antonio, Texas home improvement big box store. I set up a meeting with the CEO of Kmart and Bernie Marcus in the office of the CEO of American Express, Jim Robinson, who was always helpful to me. During the meeting Joe Antonini, Kmart's CEO, said he would continue to bet on Builders Square, and he thanked us for our time. But when we left the meeting, Bernie said to me that Builders Square would never make it, and here's why.

He said that as a business practice, Home Depot would try ten new products in ten new stores and, as a result of the test, they might roll out one or two of those products into all Home Depot stores. He then told me that, at the same time, the buyers of Builders Square would come in and see all ten new products and immediately buy all ten of them for all their stores. He explained that it was this kind of behavior that got a business into serious trouble.

Well, guess what? Just a few years later, Builders Square was out of business, and Home Depot did not sell and continues to grow. Today the stock is worth more than $300 a share with a market cap of $344.5 billion, and the company's revenue is just shy of $150 billion annually.

But as far as Sears and Kmart, two companies that have failed tremendously, it's very frustrating. You think you have a good, potentially business-saving merger, but the management won't listen. It makes me sad to see these one-time giants fail and fade. At least I get to be happy for Bernie.

IDENTIFY YOUR FRIENDS AND STICK WITH THEM

When a company goes bankrupt, it can either reorganize to a smaller scale, get rid of debt, close stores and reduce inventory, bring in new capital, and then grow again. Or, the company has failed, will no longer exist, and has to sell off all of its assets, including inventory and leases, to pay off its creditors. That's when a liquidator comes in. The liquidator goes in and appraises the company's assets and gives a price on which they're willing to liquidate—could be a base price or it could be a price with a commission, there are any number of ways to do it—and they would bring in teams of people, take over the stores, goods would disappear, and the cash would come in.

Jerry Schottenstein was exceptional at this. He would do everything possible to win the deal either as part of his group or together with other people in a consortium. He would sell the inventory to wrap up on Chapter 11 filings that would typically go on and on. Jerry was known as a very tough negotiator. However, in those days, "Your word was your bond." If you shook hands on a deal, you really didn't need paperwork (although, of course, it was done). Sadly, Jerry passed away and his son, Jay, became the major focus of the business, and we looked at a number of situations for him to buy. At the time, besides having the liquidation business, Jay owned Value City Department Stores, which was an off-price discount department store chain, and he had about a billion or two of commercial real estate.

Before I was at Lehman, I had been working with Don Fisher to buy a company in Pittsburgh that had two divisions, one of which was American Eagle Outfitters. The company was going bankrupt, but the deal with Don did not go through. Then Jay came in and acquired it. It was small. He brought in people to try and change it. It was the start of something that would put them on a great path. Today it's a $4 billion company.

Jay placed me on the board of American Eagle. As a board member, I gave advice, not only on retailing in general, but also about acquisitions and other financial matters. We looked at a number of potential companies. We talked about how to build American Eagle, both internally and externally. Internally, they were opening stores, and they were very early into social media, and their e-commerce business grew significantly to about 35 percent of its sales (which has been a lifesaver, especially during the COVID-19 pandemic). In the meantime, besides working with American Eagle, I collaborated with Jay on other things, including liquidations. One of the more interesting ones was Best Products, a catalog company that was originally a leader in its field but fell on hard times and went bankrupt. We competed in Richmond, Virginia, to do the liquidation, which turned out to be an amazing opportunity. Jay's liquidation business—Schottenstein, Bernstein—was based in New York. David Bernstein, Jay's partner, did amazing amounts of work, and we did a number of deals together.

"I have known Gilbert a long time," says Jay Schottenstein. "I first met him when he was a friend of my father's. After my father's passing, Gilbert was extremely helpful in teaching and guiding me in how to negotiate different deals. Gilbert's connections opened up a lot of doors for my businesses. When Gilbert was working on a deal, there was no one more focused than he on getting the deal done successfully."

And look, when it comes to the Schottensteins, I could go on and on as far as deals. But the fact is, early on, the Schottensteins and I realized how much we liked one another. Yes, I enjoyed doing business with them, and they enjoyed doing business with me. And when you find someone that you work well with in these highly sophisticated, pressurized situations, recognize how rare that is—indeed, how hard it is to find this out there in the shark tank of doing deals—and treat it with the kind of respect and awe that will give it a chance to last a lifetime.

LESSONS FROM TAKEOVERS

In the late seventies, we were on retainer with American Sterilizer which, at the time, was the largest company in medical equipment. We had bought many companies for them, including a contact lens company and a rehab company, among others, which allowed for them to diversify. However, one day a group approached American Sterilizer in an effort to takeover or change the company (and did so for reasons I never knew, since American Sterilizer was doing well). This was my first experience in the takeover arena and I knew little of what to do. At the time, our closest relationship was with Goldman Sachs and they were most helpful in referring us the smaller deals and we would call them when there was something bigger. American Sterilizer fit the bill and I called Steve Friedman who was then the head of mergers (he would later become their CEO). He then set up a meeting with the legendary Joe Flom (who, as mentioned, would later became a good friend). But in those days, everyone was a novice and to sit in a meeting with the lawyers at Skadden's office with the CEO of American Sterilizer was a learning experience. And honestly, though I hate to say this, it was much like the blind leading the blind, since these were the very early days of takeovers and both the lawyers and the bankers had to figure out the next moves to thwart a party and everyone was figuring out how to go about the process. Anyway, we were successful with American Sterilizer, and the hostile group went away.

With more experience, both Skadden Arps and Goldman became experts in the field of takeovers. But what Skadden did moving forward was one of the smartest things I have ever seen. Since many of the companies they met with were from outside of New York and did not have sophisticated lawyers, Skadden convinced these clients to pay a large retainer for their "protection" against unwanted suitors while at the same time allowing those companies to use their firm for other services. And, this was how they built Skadden Arps into one of the largest firms in the country.

I could go on and on about takeovers, greenmail, activism—certainly over the years, we participated in many takeover situations, mostly representing the "good guys," since we did not want to hurt our reputation—but I thought this very early experience was especially interesting and one which no one should forget for it was yet another example of how smart people take on new situations and thereby survive and prosper.

INVESTMENT BANKING AND FINANCIAL ADVISORY FEES

Perhaps forty years ago or so, a deal of $40 million was announced in the *Wall Street Journal* where we were named as the investment banker. One of my mother's friends said to her that she should be happy as I must have made 10 percent or $4 million on the deal. My mother thought her son was now very rich. When she told me as much, I laughed and straightened her out.

Of course, for anyone in the service industry, compensation is their lifeblood. In other industries, when the cash register rings, one does not necessarily need to be there to receive the income. In the legal practice as well as many other professions, however, it is normal to charge by the hour, while the youngest associates receive a much smaller amount than the partners since the associates' pay includes their base, overhead, and the partner's profit. Investment and financial advisory firms work somewhat differently as most will charge a percentage of the deal.

The usual fee for an investment banker is a percentage of the value of the deal, usually based on the amount paid for the company, less any debt, plus any excess cash. This is called the enterprise value. Initially, deals were based on the Lehman formula which was used by most other firms which was a percent of 5-4-3-2-1 of the value (that is, 5 percent of the first million, 4 percent of the second, 3 percent of the third, and so on). However, over a certain amount, say, $100 million, the fee would then be a percentage of the deal. That number would be negotiated but would usually hover in the 1 percent range. I did not like this system because the fee on smaller deals did not reflect that private companies were much harder to negotiate and sell than the larger public company. Indeed, oftentimes, the smaller companies did not have good financials and many times no outside independent accountants. The financials would have to be updated, and the owners had typically taken out a lot of fringes which needed to be added back—and all of this took a lot of time and due diligence. In the process of doing due diligence, I always asked my clients to tell me about any surprises or things hidden in the closet. If I knew of these in advance, it would be easier to explain to the buyer than if they were discovered during due diligence. Worse yet, if a surprise had not been disclosed during the negotiation, and the potential buyer discovered this, we would have enormous problems. The trust would be gone, and many times, the buyer would walk and sell to another party.

After looking at the Lehman formula, however, I decided that for my firm, I would change this up and charge a fee based on the initial prices as well as a unique sliding scale of my own devising. As an example, on a smaller deal of $20 million, we would discuss a fee of $350,000 for the first $5 million and then a sliding scale of 5-3-1 percent on each $5 million increment up to $1 million if the deal was less than $100 million. As a result, with my formula, the fee would be $470,000 as opposed to $300,000 on the Lehman formula. However, if the deal was, say, $40 million, the fee would be $670,000 as opposed to $610,000 under the Lehman formula, just narrowing the gap. As noted above, on deals of over $100 million, the fee might be 1 percent and perhaps a bonus over a certain amount. And with deals over $500 million, we would have a total negotiation to figure out the right number.

Remember, in the earlier years, the $1 billion and $20 billion deals were few and far between. When we did both the Marshalls (1995) and Hasbro-Milton Bradley deals (1984), which were both in the $500 million range, they were in the top 10 percent of deals done that year.

Today, deals in the hundreds of millions of dollars would not even garner a mention in the business pages.

Furthermore, we also decided to charge an initial retainer and add additional retainers at different stages of the negotiations so that should a deal fall apart, die, or get topped, we would still receive some remuneration for the time we had invested. Originally, it was more difficult to get a retainer of $500 or $1,000 as compared to a retainer of $50,000 to $100,000 today. I have to thank Bob Gallagher, one of the head partners at Bache & Co. in the 1970s, then one of the predominant investment banking firms, for suggesting we charge a retainer. We were new to the business then, and he was with a major firm where many never charged retainers since they had brokerage and other trading income to compensate for the failure of a deal. But retainers were very important in my mind because they committed us to the client and the client to us.

Many may ask, "Why such high fees?" The answer is simple: for every deal one does, there may be five, ten, or more deals that do not go anywhere. In a given year, we might have done ten deals or perhaps as many as thirty, but we would have spent time on twice that number. We had to ensure that we were compensated for that time too. We value all our time, every last minute. It must all be compensated for.

HAVE I MENTIONED THE SOUP AND NUTS OF A DEAL?

When a company is interested in selling its business or divesting a division or subsidiary, I have always taken the position that retaining an investment banker or financial advisor is essential. It gives the seller protection and allows for them to be one step removed from the potential buyer. It also allows me and my other bankers to play good cop, bad cop as the client must *always* be right. Of course, when I say the prospective client must or *should* retain the banker, many think the only reason I say this is because of the fee that I will receive for my work. But that is not true. Just as a surgeon would not operate on himself, we do not endorse foregoing a lawyer or financial advisor trained in our line of work. Serious injury—this, of a financial nature—can and will result.

The seller should always interview more than one investment banker or financial advisor. This helps them choose the right one to do the deal. They should explore the expertise in the type of business of which the seller is engaged, the reputation and creditability (and credibility) of the banking firm, the knowledge of the individual banker involved and, most important of all, the chemistry between the seller and the banker. In many cases, we have been lucky because several clients that have used us before will return to do a second or third deal. It shows loyalty, commitment, and that we can get a deal done together, while also speaking to a strong chemistry between all parties.

During my career, we have participated in many "beauty" contests where the seller will interview more than one banker and look at each of their qualifications. They may also give the banker some initial financials and other information on the business and ask them to give a range of values for the business. We have seen things done during this process which gave us cause for concern. For example, to get the assignment, one of the competing bankers might give a value in a range so high that the deal could never possibly get done at that price. The price is attractive, yes, but totally unrealistic. We have always tried to give a reasonable range of the seller's value and have lost business because of higher values given by competing firms. In many and most cases, when the business is finally sold, the price is closer to what we originally proposed. Unsurprisingly, we lost the business and the competitor got the fee. Although frustrating, we still do not inflate our numbers but try to always be on the level and realistic with a prospective client—our credibility and reputation is at stake. While being smart is critical, one must maintain their credibility and reputation to survive.

Also, when choosing the banker, it is important to know exactly who will work on the deal. Many firms will bring a senior banker to the presentations and imply that they will lead the deal when in fact, there is a "bait and switch," and a junior banker without the necessary knowledge does all the work. The client never sees the senior banker again until the closing when the fee is paid.

Once retained, we or another banker put together a list of needed materials for the client and spend time meeting with them, reviewing all the documents, and getting information, not only on the base business, but also the financials and any other pertinent details.

Upon a decision to retain the banker, a fee agreement needs to be negotiated, but it is essential that it be put in writing. In the early days, a handshake would be all that was needed but as the deals became more complicated, a written agreement became essential to prevent any misunderstandings. Part of any retention would be a confidentiality agreement, which is essential and sometimes limited to those in the banker's firm who would have any knowledge of the deal, especially in the most sensitive of matters.

As discussed earlier, fees for deals take on a flavor of their own and can differ substantially depending on the deal and its size and nature. The important thing is to have the fee and engagement agreement signed so there will be no misunderstandings, which can lead to conflict at a time when the banker and seller need to be aligned. (I have already discussed the range of fees earlier in this book.)

Upon retention, the banker needs to meet with the client, discuss and understand the business, review initial financials and business materials, and meet the executives of the company (unless secrecy is required to keep things confidential). After the initial review, the banker must discuss their thoughts on the value of the transaction and discuss a possible list of buyers whether strategic or financial. Also, in many cases, competitors of the seller may be excluded as potential buyers as it could hurt the seller's business in the interim.

As mentioned earlier, one thing we always asked our clients was whether there were any surprises. This was critical because when the potential buyer started doing their own due diligence it would always come out. No business is 100 percent perfect. We always tell the client that if we don't know the problem and it was found out, the potential buyer would wonder what additional problems were being covered up. This is probably the most important thing we did to protect our clients' creditability. And many times, if not disclosed at the right time, the deal would end up dying.

When dealing with private, family-owned companies as opposed to public companies or companies owned by PE firms where there is a lot of accountability, there must be extended due diligence. In many cases, the financials are done by a smaller accounting firm, but they haven't been audited. The "owner" may take out excess salaries and expenses that are really not associated with the act of doing business. In the past, we have seen private companies have as many as ten personal cars on the books, a plane, a yacht, and in one case, a housekeeper. This can lead to an add-back to reconcile the amount on the financials to reflect the going-forward financial earnings of the business. Moreover, businesses will have family members on the payroll that cannot be justified, and the buyer may not believe that those are the only discrepancies. This can also lead to tax problems, which can affect both the buyer and the seller. Therefore, it all needs to be made transparent.

The due diligence and investigation of a company progresses with such measures as meetings with the management teams, visits to stores, warehouses, and executive offices, discussions about how to proceed in talking to potential parties, the sharing of information, negotiations, and the preparation of a selling document which is usually called the Confidential Memorandum. In some cases, the document will include all relevant information on the company. In others, just a preliminary scope of material is given to allow the prospective buyer to express interest with a letter of intent. This allows the seller to review potential bids before opening the "barn door" to all the parties. Thereafter, one or two parties may be selected to move into the second round, and in many cases, a "data room" will be opened, which contains a lot more detailed information to be reviewed as part of the buyer's due diligence. In my early days as a banker, the data room would be a room in our office or the lawyer's, but not in the seller's facilities in order to keep things confidential. This would include boxes upon boxes of documents, leases, and other pertinent information. Today, all of this data room material is digitized, which makes the process easier and more efficient.

Negotiations are an essential part of the process and can have many different forms. They may include all of the parties or a smaller group of them, as well as back-and-forth meetings with us working separately with the individual parties. Like a cat, a deal can have many different lives and can live or die a day at a time. Being too laid back or too pushy can make or break a deal. The negotiations may go quickly, or they may go on for months or even years, which would probably kill the deal as, during this time, the value of the business might change.

We had a deal with a most famous beauty company that was going to buy another beauty company. The deal went on for eighteen months and died. During this period, the offer went up and down, as did the earnings. We initially offered sixteen dollars a share when the price was nine dollars a share, a substantial premium, but the seller wanted twenty-five dollars a share, a prohibitively high sum. Then the earnings dropped, and the CEO left the firm. The parent company of the seller said we could buy the company for the original offer of sixteen dollars a share, but then we thought it to be worth less than ten dollars a share. So, in what could have been a game changer in the industry, the deal died. Today, the company is still in business but worth nowhere near as much.

Assuming the negotiations are successful and the acquisition agreement is signed, the closing then takes place. They may be simple or a huge affair.

So, the deal is done, but now comes an announcement and press release in which, hopefully, the banker is included. That is very important to us, as it adds to our creditability and gives us another notch on our belt.

CLOSINGS

A deal may be signed, but unless it closes, all is lost. I always used the expression, "It's not over 'til the fat lady sings."

We had many closings that were simple and just required a visit to the lawyer's offices or sometimes by mail with none of us present. Other times, the closings were exciting and something to remember. We would schedule a dinner at the Four Seasons or other top venues where both sides—the principals, the lawyers, the bankers, and others—would attend. There would be congratulatory comments and gifts and sometimes gag gifts as well. At the Stuart Weitzman closing, Stuart made a size fourteen shoe to give to his new partner at Irving Capital and made him wear it and walk around the room. Always, the client would want the investment banker to pay the bills, and we gladly did it either ourselves or jointly with the other banker.

While we went on boats and to interesting venues, perhaps the most exciting closing I ever experienced was the closing of the National Living Centers sale to ARA Services in 1973. This was then the largest nursing home company. They were based in Houston, and both ARA and I were based in Philadelphia. We flew to Houston on ARA's plane. In those days, private planes were much smaller than the G6s that are used by corporations today, and while the flight was good, Shelley was pregnant with Nancy, and to sit on the plane for a number of hours was very difficult for her. Moreover, in those days there were no bathrooms, only a seat with a curtain around it. Well, to her credit, Shelley endured the flight, and we arrived in Houston. The Billy Jean King/Bobby Riggs tennis match, which had been billed as the "Battle of the Sexes," was being held on that very day in the Astrodome. ARA catered the event, and one of the Directors of National Living Centers in fact owned the Astrodome. As a result, we were all invited, with front row seats, to this now-famous match. It followed with a dinner, and the next day we closed and returned to Philadelphia. A most memorable closing, indeed.

OPENING OFFICES ABROAD

As our business expanded, we would spend time traveling to see clients and negotiate deals whether to LA, San Francisco, Dallas or other parts of the US. A lot of time was spent on planes and hotels for a meeting which might take two or three hours. Early on at Financo, when Steve Klein and I were partners, Steve bought a plane and we used that for short runs with clients, especially to Erie where we did a lot of work with American Sterilizer. I often thought that it only made sense to have all of our bankers in one office where they can relate and work together as deals must be collaborative and the thoughts on one banker may help in moving a deal forward.

While I had done a lot of work outside of the US in my time at Lehman, after I left and restarted Financo, if I was working on a deal in London or Paris or somewhere else in Europe, I would get on a plane and work either in the client's office or in my suite which was usually in Claridge's, especially since I no longer used the Lehman offices there. This was very effective and clients and potential clients loved coming to this great hotel which was then, as now, a fantastic place. However, as our global business increased and we started to do more deals in London and other European cities, we realized that we could have a problem in a potential violation of the UK securities laws and that it would be necessary to register in order to do business. Chuck Lubar was helpful for getting Financo registered in the UK.

We brought in a person named David Ishag, whom I had met through Michael Milken, and he was our "man-in-town." We did a number of deals with Sears plc, Kingfisher, Top Shop, Asprey, Ratners, to name a few, and therefore, having a more permanent base outside the U.S., in this case in London, made total sense.

ON GIVING BACK

I've always believed that to be successful, you have to give back. In Philadelphia, I became the co-Chairman of the Young Israel Bonds Forum, and that led to my first trip to Israel. When I was honored by that charity, Joe Biden presented me with the award. I also became involved in the Jewish Federation of Greater Philadelphia and did fundraising for them and was on their board. Similarly, at my synagogue, Rodeph Shalom, I was on the Executive Committee. At Penn, I started the Entrepreneurial Center which led to my teaching the course on mergers that I've already mentioned. As a lecturer, each year I had a class of around fifteen handpicked students for a two hour-session each week. I brought in some of the biggest names in business at the time to speak including Saul Steinberg and Meshulam Riklis along with lawyers and accountants, all to let the students learn something about mergers. That led to my being invited onto the Board of Wharton, where such people as Saul Steinberg, Reg Jones (CEO of GE), and Jon Huntsman (CEO of The Huntsman Corporation) were the chairman over the years. I was honored to be part of this illustrious group. Incidentally, my salary as a lecturer was $2,500, but I gave that back to Penn and a lot more, having endowed a Wharton Term Professorship, a Study Hall, a Reception Area in the Executive Education Center, as well as being one of the original founders of the Penn Club in New York.

When I moved to New York, I became involved with the Fashion Institute of Technology where I eventually became co-chairman of the board. I also joined the UJA Federation of New York, where I became the chairman of their Fashion Group, which was most important to me. I became the Treasurer of the Southampton Hospital Foundation where I am also a board member of the hospital. My wife and I are also involved with the Met, MOMA and the Israel Museum. Perhaps the most fun, I was on the board of the Peggy Guggenheim Museum in Venice, which required me to go to board meetings there at least one a year, along with other venues around the world where the Guggenheim had a foothold: Bilbao, Madrid, Moscow, St. Petersburg, Israel, London, Rome, Paris, Chile, Peru, and elsewhere. It's very important to put some of your money and time into causes outside of your business life. It deepens your perspective. You see the larger picture. It all helps.

STAY FIT

As I have gotten older, health and fitness has become an important part of my life and something I do not take lightly. Although I have had a knee replacement, a hernia operation, and a ruptured disc, my hope is that I will have many more years, as I have been lucky enough to have a mother who lived until ninety-seven, a father who unfortunately died of Parkinson's disease at eighty-seven, and grandparents that lived to seventy-three, ninety-three, ninety-five, and one hundred and two. I like to think that good genes are, therefore, on my side. But it is critical to stay in good shape.

Says my longtime physical therapist, Kimberly Caspare, on the subject:

"The key to longevity is competent posture awareness, deep breathing, and a consistent focus on balance. The key to joint preservation is muscle strength. The key to staying fit for Gilbert is his pursuit of better health. His unwavering discipline to get up every morning and move is vital to his resilience. His dedication can be seen in mending the body kinks with me, pedaling away on a bike, side stroking in a pool, and in the gym with Walker where you can hear his fingers snapping to a beat as he balances on one leg."

Believe me, you can't do your job at the highest levels if you're not feeling your best. So, among all the other demands of a busy life, make sure to prioritize exercise.

COLLECTING ART

From the start of our marriage, art has been a passion for both me and Shelley. One of the first things we did with some of the money we received at our wedding was to buy a piece of art. Oh, how we agitated over buying that first piece, a Leger poster for fifty dollars. We have now probably spent one thousand-times that amount in a split moment decision. Back then, however, I was only earning $7,800-a-year. The Leger poster, as it were, was something that we "had" to have—and this has always been the way it goes. Our passion drives the purchase.

In reality, I am a very decisive person and when looking at a piece of art, I will immediately say whether or not I like it. People say I have an "eye." Shelley, on the other hand, is very methodical and does her homework. We make a good pair going about in the field and meeting people. Some dealers are insulted when I say that I do not like a piece, where others respect my honesty.

There are two lessons that I should impress. First, buy a piece of art because you love it and not for investment purposes. If the piece is good, the price may rise but loving it is more important. Second, if you love a piece of art, try not to sell it if possible as you will regret this later. Sure, you may need the funds, but if you can get the monies somewhere else, try to.

Collecting has truly enhanced our lives. We have met fantastic people, made friends with many, traveled the globe with art museum groups, in love with the search for the picture.

Gilbert at a Financo CEO conference. Bottom row from left to right: Mike Ullman (CEO of JC Penney), David Simon (CEO of Simon Properties), Mickey Drexler (CEO of J.Crew), Solomon Lew (Chairman of Just Group), Steve Sadove (CEO of Saks Fifth Avenue); top row from left to right: Manny Chirico (CEO of PVH), Matt Serra (CEO of Footlocker), Ron Frasch (President of Saks Fifth Avenue), Gilbert, Burt Transky (Chairman and CEO of Neiman Marcus), Matt Rubel (CEO of Collective Brands), and Joseph Gromek (CEO of Warnaco Group).

| CHAPTER 6 |

In the Realm of the Standout Specialty Store:
Seeing Some of the Greatest Retailers of All Time Grow Their Iconic Brands

GORDON SEGAL AND CRATE & BARREL

In 1977, I was hired by the owner of Ann Taylor stores, Richard Liebeskind, to sell Ann Taylor. One of the companies we visited first was Hart, Shaffner & Marx which was then one of the best-run men's retailers in the US. The chairman of the company met us in his office in Chicago, and he turned to Liebeskind and said, "Welcome to Chicago, Dick." Liebeskind replied, "My name is Richard." Well, the next day, I was back in Philadelphia, and the chairman called me up and said he really would have liked to have bought Ann Taylor as it would have brought him into the women's business, but he needed Liebeskind's expertise to run the company and anyone who would answer the way *he* had to being called Dick—mind you, these were the first words out of his mouth—was not someone he would want to work with. This is a lesson that stuck with me for the rest of my career. I like the name Gilbert, but if someone calls me Gil or Gilly or anything, I just smile and continue on in the moment.

Well, I ended up finding a buyer for Ann Taylor in Garfinckel, Brooks Brothers who were based in Washington DC. Just to give you a sense of how the numbers have changed over the years: Garfinckel,

Brooks Brothers only wanted to pay $5 million for Ann Taylor, and I got them up to six—20 percent more—and the $1 million difference felt substantial to all the parties involved. (On a number of occasions in the future, the company would be sold at values of up to $500 million. Unfortunately, they recently went through bankruptcy).

After the sale, Richard Liebeskind continued on as president of Ann Taylor, and we would meet from time to time to discuss potential opportunities. Liebeskind had opened his first Ann Taylor location in my hometown of New Haven back in 1954. So, in addition to working on the sale of Ann Taylor and bringing it across the finish, he and I shared a past with the New Haven of the 1950s.

Next to the Ann Taylor location in Boston's Faneuil Hall was a business out of Chicago with only a few stores to its name called Crate & Barrel. Liebeskind introduced me to the Crate & Barrel founder, Gordon Segal. Right away, it was obvious to me that Gordon had a fantastic mind, was a great merchant, and that he was going to grow his company. We became friends.

Come this time, Ken Walker and I were already having our dinners at the Four Seasons Hotel during the National Retail Federation Convention, and, as mentioned earlier, Gordon would always be among the attendees. It seemed like every time we saw one another, his company had grown bigger and bigger. He wouldn't have taken any huge steps to grow it either. He moved slowly, methodically. Here's a very telling quote from Gordon in the American Home Furnishings Hall of Fame Oral History:

> "All of our money was in the business. We had never taken any money out of the business. Everything was at risk with every big expansion."

For Gordon, growth was all about taking his time and building it up one block at a time. But you couldn't ignore the fact that the company was becoming bigger and more dominant. And because of that, naturally, I would talk to him about selling Crate & Barrel. I saw so many opportunities—great ones—should he wish to sell. But again and again, he told me no. He didn't want to.

However, as Gordon said in the American Home Furnishing Hall of Fame interview:

"We were behind our big competitors...We thought about going public, but I wasn't sure I wanted to do that since I didn't want to be criticized when bad years and bad seasons came along. I also didn't want to be overly cautious. As merchants, we always took a lot of chances, tried new ideas and new products, and we'd have good seasons and bad seasons. I didn't know if I wanted to have to sit there and explain it all to some young Wall Street analysts. It's also my personality that I just don't want the whole world to see how we're doing. I didn't like the idea of going public. We looked for partners. We interviewed a lot of people for a year and a half..."

About this time, in 1997, I was talking to Don Fisher at the Gap, as I would see him periodically in New York or in California, and Don asked me to try and get Gordon Segal interested in talking to him.

So, the Gap retained me to buy Crate & Barrel—and that did it, with the Gap onboard, now Gordon *was* interested.

We started to have meetings, in New York, in Chicago, in California, and they were going well. But some of the people at the Gap convinced Don not to do the deal because they thought Crate & Barrel had peaked. Anyway, that was that. The deal was off the table.

I now had all of these insights into Crate & Barrel—all the information, the numbers—and Gordon was still looking to sell. As I had been representing the Gap in the deal for Crate & Barrel, Gordon had acquired his own investment banker, and he couldn't throw them under the bus. But Gordon was a friend, and even though I was out of the deal, I wouldn't turn my back on him; I'd help find him a buyer for Crate & Barrel.

So, I thought of different people and Invest Corp, the Middle East buyout firm, was doing a lot of buyout deals then, so I spoke to Savio Tung there. He was very interested. We had meetings. Tung put together a proposal to buy Crate & Barrel in the $400 million range, which in those days was a lot of money. However, there were two things that they let Gordon know would happen should they buy him out that didn't quite sit right with him: one, they'd highly leverage Crate & Barrel. And two, at the end of three to five years, they'd either sell the business or take it public. After all, Invest Corp was a private equity firm, and that's what private equity firms do. Well, neither of these options appealed to Gordon. So the deal fell apart.

Meanwhile, the Otto Group was also very interested in Crate & Barrel. They came in and offered slightly less than Invest Corp had. However, they were willing to buy 60–70 percent for cash, with no leverage, and leave Gordon with a nice percentage of the company and no debt. Gordon took the deal. To his own amazement, as well as my own, Gordon sold the rest of Crate & Barrel years later to the Otto Group and received more for the remaining 30–40 percent than he did when he sold the front half to them.

And me? Because I know you're wondering, what did I get in the deal? I earned no commission, no fee other than the retainer from the Gap. But it was an experience that solidified my friendship with Gordon, someone I respect and hold dear. He is one of the great Merchant Princes—and for that reason, in the end, it was a terrific deal for me.

DON FISHER AND THE GAP

Speaking of the Gap again, I had a very interesting relationship with Don Fisher, the founder and CEO of the company, and also Mickey Drexler, the retail whiz and their one-time president. I had met Mickey when he was leaving Ann Taylor, which, at the time, was owned by Allied Department Stores. Mickey didn't like Tom Macioce, who was the CEO of Allied. Yes, Macioce gave Mickey a lot of problems, so he decided to seek greener pastures.

I was very close to AEA Investors, a buyout firm that had done our deal with Shoe Town as well as Loehmann's. I was having dinner with Mickey Drexler and Michel Zaleski from AEA to discuss how we could find a business for Mickey to run that AEA would acquire. Mickey was very excited about it, as was I. Mickey was brilliant, and the job of finding a great fit for him with the kind of company that needed a good boost—well, that's my idea of a good time. However, in the middle of our conversation, somewhere between the appetizers and the main course, Mickey said that despite his enthusiasm for our plans, we'd have to wait a week to get down to more serious talks. Turns out, Mickey had promised a headhunter that he'd go out to San Francisco to meet Don Fisher of the Gap. Mickey told us that there was no way that his family was going to move out to San Francisco from New York, so we should definitely expect this conversation to pick up after his return. We asked him what if he changed his mind and said yes to Don. But again, Mickey insisted that there was no chance that that would happen.

Well, it makes me laugh now because, of course, you know the rest of the story. Mickey went to the Gap and transformed the company into one of the largest specialty stores in the world. You've got to give Mickey a lot of credit for his time there. His work was nothing less than extraordinary. (And then he did it again in transforming J.Crew.)

But Mickey, while focused on the clothes, the branding, and real estate, didn't necessarily love the kinds of conversations I'd have with Don wherein I'd try and bring his attention to an acquisition that might help grow the business. It's what I do, and I do it aggressively and unapologetically. But what's interesting is that when I talked to Don in the past about taking him private, Don said he wouldn't do it because he didn't want the debt hanging over him. He wanted to grow the company instead—and that he certainly did.

But in 1984, before the Crate & Barrel opportunity, I was speaking with Don about an acquisition that he finally went ahead with, and that was for Pottery Barn.

Pottery Barn was a small company selling homewear in New York. At the time, they had between five and ten stores. Don felt that a home products line would complement the Gap and that his team could work magic in terms of growing the business.

In his memoir, *"Falling Into the Gap,"* Don said:

> "I asked Gilbert to find out if Pottery Barn might entertain an offer to their business. Gilbert got right on the case and found enough interest to set up an appointment for me with the company's owner, Hoyt Chapin. I met with Hoyt and liked him immediately. He was very unassuming and open, and told me straight up that he'd thought about selling out and maybe retiring..."

In Hoyt Chapin, you had a person who was ready to get out of a business that he had made a lot of money running, someone who was ready to step away and do something else with his life. And, in Don, you had someone who was at the height of his success, looking to continue to grow his company. What followed was a successful first meeting between Don and Hoyt. Shortly thereafter, they would meet again, and following "a relatively easy negotiation," in Don's words, the Gap bought Pottery Barn for $20 million.

Unfortunately, at the end of a year, the Gap had lost $1.4 million in its Pottery Barn businesses. The synergies weren't working out the way they should have been, and Don wasn't convinced that he could turn the business around, so he decided to sell.

"I wondered," said Don, in his memoir, "how many times [Gilbert Harrison and Financo] got involved in selling a business to someone, only to sell the same business again, for whatever reasons, a short time later."

Well, these things do happen. And we turned around and sold Pottery Barn to another San Francisco based company, William Sonoma, who did amazing things with the brand and has had great success. So, as you can see, it wasn't that Pottery Barn didn't have the potential to be the giant that it is, but they had to be aligned with the right company. And, in this case, we didn't have it right with the Gap. It was an easy deal to make, but one that didn't quite work out. Happily, the CEO of Pottery Barn, Gary Friedman, did a great job to make the company a dominant force and is doing the same a second time around with Restoration Hardware.

JOS. A. BANK AND MEN'S WEARHOUSE FIGHT TO THE DEATH

In an article on January 17th, 2014, Rachel Abrams of the *New York Times* referred to t
he "never-ending takeover war between two of the country's largest men's suit retailers": Jos A. Bank and Men's Wearhouse.

Indeed, as I was representing Jos A. Bank in the deal, I would be the first to tell you that things were taking a very long time to get done. But some deals are like that. Some deals take a very long time, and you have to be extremely patient. This was one of those situations that had a million twists and turns, and it simply had to go through each and every one of them before it could get across the finish line.

Thirty-two years earlier, in *Men's Wear*, I said:

"Every deal has nine lives. They all fall apart at some point in the negotiations, and it is the good dealmaker who can put them back together. This is intuitive and can't be taught."

Honestly, this deal had a hundred lives, and intuition went out the window early. This was unchartered territory. For its number of burials and rebirths, I had never seen anything like it before, and I haven't seen anything like it since.

At the time, Jos. A. Bank was probably the most profitable of the tailor-clothing retailers and had built up cash reserves of half a billion dollars. I had known the chairman, Bob Wildrick, for many years, having first met him long before when he was the executive vice-president of Belk Department Stores, as I had done work with the company's chairman, John Belk. I saw the way Bob had grown Jos. A. Bank. When he took over in 1999, the company reported losses of $13.2 million. But two years later, they were already reporting a profit of some $2.5 million. Bob continued to do great by them, building extremely strong infrastructure, sourcing, design, and construction departments. In 2003, Bob also started a very strong e-commerce business for the company. And by 2013, the company had a market capitalization of $900 million, and they had about $400 million in cash with no debt. But they saw that their business, in terms of growth, was starting to flatten out. All companies are in various stages of growth. There's the growth curve, beginning with the initial startup position, and then the dominance, and finally the leveling off and downturn. Once the leveling off starts to come, to resist a downturn, a company must make a decision whether to sell or use its cash and other reserves to acquire a similar company where they can use their abilities to grow a new but related business—and this is where Jos. A. Bank found itself.

We put together a list of probably twenty or thirty targets, a number of companies we felt would make sense for Jos. A. Bank to buy, and we approached them. For starters, Lucky Jeans, Brooks Brothers, and Vineyard Vines.

Lucky Jeans could have been an interesting company. It was having problems, and it was for sale. We flew to California to meet with them, and we had a good meeting. But Bob Wildrick decided to pass on the deal for two reasons. The first was that the management was what we call "intertwined." What do I mean by intertwined? In this case, the CEO had a life-partner who was in charge of all new stores. He was making a salary of about $500,000 a year, and he was terrible at his job. We knew that if we fired the life-partner, the CEO would walk, and this was problematic. The second issue was that this same CEO really didn't like operating in a business climate like the one that existed in California. Of course, should a deal be made, Lucky Jeans wasn't going to relocate so that this CEO could be made happy. And so, with all of that in mind, Bob said, "Forget Lucky Jeans."

Next, we had Vineyard Vines in our sights. The company would have been a great fit because it was doing better and better and really had a good sense of where it was heading. Not surprisingly, even though we offered a substantial amount of money, the owners decided to keep the business and grow it themselves.

Brooks Brothers became our next favorite choice because Jos. A. Bank could use its management ability and develop a "better-best" format with Brooks Brother being the "best" and Jos. A. Bank being the more moderate tier. The price became a sticking point. Claudio Del Vecchio wanted $1.4 billion. We felt that it was probably worth closer to a billion. We went back and forth, but we couldn't agree on a number, and Brooks Brothers was out. (PS: Brooks Brothers recently went bankrupt, and Del Vecchio lost the business to Authentic Brands Group, which has a history of buying up struggling branded companies.)

Then one day, the paper reported there were significant management problems at Men's Wearhouse, Jos. A Banks's main competitor. From the *Guardian*, July 27th, 2013:

"The former face of retailer Men's Wearhouse has denied 'ego' was behind the high-profile row that saw him ousted from the company he founded."

Since the 1990s, George Zimmer has told potential customers 'You'll like the way you look. I guarantee it,' in nationwide ads for the men's retail chain. The gravelly-voiced Zimmer quit the company's board earlier this month after the company terminated his role as executive chairman.

In an open letter, Zimmer wrote that he was abruptly fired so that the company could appoint a new board 'that excluded me.'

'To justify their actions, they now have tried to portray me as an obstinate former CEO, determined to regain absolute control by pushing a going private transaction for my own benefit and ego,' wrote Zimmer. 'Nothing could be further from the truth.'"

As you can see, there were tensions. The founder of the company was out, and the management was in crisis. Jos. A. Bank could come in and quite possibly right the ship. The one catch: Men's Wearhouse wasn't for sale. We knew it. But we didn't care. We were going to go after Men's Wearhouse.

We put together a team to research the company, and we brought in Skadden Arps as the lawyer, and Goldman Sachs to help with the financing because there was just no way that Financo could have done a deal that raised the $2.5 billion needed to buy this company. We were going to work equally with Goldman then, but they would be in charge of raising the capital that was needed. We put together information. We made an approach, which, unsurprisingly, Men's Wearhouse rejected. We danced back and forth. We gave them a bear hug letter, which they also rejected. We sent additional letters to them in which we continued to try and get them to bite. Then they resorted to a Pac Man Defense. You've played the video game before? If so, then maybe you can guess that a Pac Man Defense is when you're going after somebody and suddenly they turn around and go after you. It's unexpected, it's dramatic and aggressive. But now we were the company being pursued with Men's Wearhouse trying to buy Jos. A. Bank for $1.5 billion. We listened to their offer, yes, but we felt that it wasn't adequate. At the same time, we thought that maybe we would make a counteroffer of our own. But it's a game. In other words, when all is said and done, these moves are like a game. And at some point, perhaps they would give in or perhaps we would give in. Understandably, in all deals that are unfriendly, there's always a narrative tension, and nobody knows who to believe or who not to believe and what games they're playing. I said earlier that when you're buying or selling a company, you try to figure out what the other party's objectives are. Do they really want to sell? Are they negotiating for a higher price? Can they not stand the people? I mean, there are a hundred different reasons why tensions arise. But in this case, it was just very difficult to know anyone's true motivations. All we knew was that things were really dragging on.

And now, Bob Wildrick, the CEO of Jos. A. Bank, wasn't sure whether it made sense to merge with Men's Wearhouse at the price they had offered. He still wanted to remain independent. Perhaps he'd rather buy a company that he could grow and run himself, but he was always looking to do what was best for his shareholders. While we had looked at Brooks Brothers and Vineyard Vines and so on, we realized that they weren't worth pursuing. Eddie Bauer was an interesting company because it was sportswear, and it complimented Jos. A. Bank. Also, it was owned by a private equity firm, it was available, and it hadn't grown as much as it should have in its hey-day and had no real direction. I had known the company for many years while it was part of the Otto Group. At that time, I was on the board of American Eagle Outfitters, who wanted to buy a company that would target customers as they outgrew the American Eagle product line. We had identified Eddie Bauer then because it was having problems, and they had entered into discussions to acquire it. Unfortunately, a deal did not go through because the Otto Group refused to sell the company.

But here we were again, fighting through this drawn-out negotiation between Jos. A. Bank and Men's Wearhouse. We were starting to ask whether we were going to get anyplace with them. Did Eddie Bauer give us an alternative? Bob Wildrick thought he and his team could turn Eddie Bauer around. Eddie Bauer had casual clothes which would balance out the tailored clothes that were in Jos. A. Bank. So, do you want to buy Eddie Bauer and forget about Men's Wearhouse? Do you want to use the Eddie Bauer deal to defer? Has Eddie Bauer become a poison pill? Do you want to deter Men's Wearhouse from going forward because this would cost them another three, four, five hundred million dollars if we also owned Eddie Bauer? And, at this point, we were getting tired.

Well, we decided to go after Eddie Bauer, and we entered into an agreement to buy the company. When we did this, Men's Wearhouse got upset, because now they were officially trying to buy Jos. A. Bank. They were getting the financing together, and they saw that the addition of Eddie Bauer to Jos. A. Bank would be an impediment to the purchase. And so, they sued to try to stop the acquisition.

In the *New York Times*, dated February 24, 2014, Rachel Abrams wrote:

> "The hostile takeover battle between Men's Wearhouse and Jos. A. Bank Clothiers just grew even more heated…As part of its lawsuit on Monday, Men's Wearhouse demanded that Jos. A. Bank rescind its poison pill threshold. It also said that the plan to buy Eddie Bauer was not a 'bona fide' corporate acquisition as part of a long-term plan.
>
> 'In fact, the Eddie Bauer transaction has little to do with the long-term welfare of JOSB, and has everything to do with the short-term interest of the JOSB board—dominated by its longtime chairman, Robert Wildrick—to remain in control and fend off an unwanted suitor,' the lawsuit said, using the stock ticker symbol for Jos. A. Bank.
>
> Men's Wearhouse also criticized the proposed Eddie Bauer acquisition for having 'almost no synergies' with Jos. A. Bank, and cited analysts who had called the deal 'totally off the wall.'"

That was their position. Of course, it was not ours. We were looking for alternatives in a deal that had gone on and on and on. Or, as it was put at the time in *USA TODAY*, Jos. A. Bank had simply decided to go "casual":

"The men's clothing retailer said Friday it has agreed to buy Eddie Bauer for about $825 million, a move to ward off a take-over bid from a competitor and diversify its product lines beyond suits, tuxedos, and work attire.

Eddie Bauer has struggled for years with brand identity, shifting from its heritage of outdoor and sportswear to dressier products and home goods like table linens. It switched its focus back to outdoor wear in the early 2000s but lost momentum and sales to competitors like Land's End, L.L. Bean, and J.Crew.

With plans to add stores and expand globally, the combined company is expected to generate more than $2.1 billion in revenue in 2014, Jos. A. Bank estimated."

We were feeling good about things. This was a great move for Jos. A. Bank after having tried to acquire another company to grow the brand for a long time. But we couldn't celebrate yet. Wouldn't you know it, the deal was held up in court and eventually thwarted by a judge. Men's Wearhouse then upped their offer to $1.8 billion if we dropped the purchase of Eddie Bauer. As far as we were concerned, the offer had been sweetened and Jos. A. Bank was willing to accept it.

From the *Washington Post* on March 11, 2014:

"Men's Wearhouse agreed to buy Maryland-based Jos. A. Bank on Tuesday in a deal worth $1.8 billion [16-18 times EBITDA] ending nearly six months of public hostilities between the menswear retailers.

The combined company will become the country's fourth-largest men's retailer, with $3.5 billion a year in sales and more than 1,700 stores across the country, Men's Wearhouse and Jos. A. Bank said in a joint statement. Jos. A. Bank's brand will stay independent, they said.

Tuesday's announcement comes a week after the retailers began negotiating and caps months of public bickering.

The companies, which have competed for budget-conscious customers for years, said Tuesday that they were better off working together. Jos. A. Bank is known for its frequent sales, including 'Buy 1 Suit, Get 3 Free' offers, while Men's Wearhouse promotes itself as a year-round low-cost alternative. Jos. A. Bank has said that customers were becoming immune to its promotions.

Both companies issued statements absent of any of the recent acrimony.

'We are pleased to have reached this agreement with Jos. A. Bank, which we believe will deliver substantial benefits to our respective shareholders, employees and customers,' Doug Ewert, president and chief executive of Men's Wearhouse, said in a statement."

So, at long last, the two companies moved on together. And, it wasn't all bad for Eddie Bauer. They had an "out clause" in the deal that we had been putting together that said that if we didn't close, Jos. A. Bank would have to pay Eddie Bauer $25 million as a walk-away fee. When Men's Wearhouse bought Jos. A. Bank and rejected the Eddie Bauer deal, the shareholders of Eddie Bauer got $25 million. But for Men's Wearhouse and Jos. A. Bank, the deal ended up being a disaster because of the management of Men's Wearhouse, who had no interest in Jos. A. Bank employees. From the beginning, Men's Wearhouse management wasn't even open to meeting Bob Wildrick or myself or listening to the plans that he and I had put together about how to integrate and run the combined companies. As a result of this, the company floundered and went bankrupt, and all of the Men's Warehouse shareholder value was lost.

When Bob took over Jos. A. Banks, it had a market capitalization of less than $18 million. Thirteen years later, the company was sold for $1.8 billion—more than one hundred times as much. This was the result of Bob's work. He was able to build a very strong company but, more importantly, he never lost sight of his fiduciary responsibilities, and he never let his ego get in the way of doing the right thing for his shareholders and employees at all levels.

"I consider Gilbert one of the smartest and most knowledgeable strategic advisors that I have met in my long career," says Bob Wildrick. "While the final deal was very important, people should be aware that for many years before, I would call Gilbert to discuss other strategic opportunities, and he always gave me good advice that I used more often than he knows."

To that extent, aside from mergers and acquisitions, we discussed many things that allowed the business to grow including the ability to go on television with fifteen-second spots which resulted in dramatically increased sales and also allowed Jos. A. Bank to grow beyond being just a regional retailer and become a retailer known through the country. Perhaps even as important, Bob and I had long discussions concerning the internet and, in 2002, Jos. A. Bank was, without a doubt, one of the first companies to recognize its importance and aggressively develop their new areas of business.

Of all the clients I've had during my long career, Bob and I had the right chemistry which resulted in a relationship that I have had with very few other clients, and our experiences together provided many life lessons, perhaps some of the *most* important of my whole career.

Gilbert, the consummate world traveler, always mixing business with pleasure.

| CHAPTER 7 |

Letting Go:
The Sale of Financo and My Final
Days at the Company I Had Built

THE YEAR WAS 2012. I had recently brought in Colin Welch to be President of Financo. Colin was an investment banker that I had originally met when he was at J.P. Morgan. We had worked on various transactions together, and I had gotten to know him. He'd had an offer from Lehman Brothers to run their retail group in Europe and moved there with his family. When Lehman Brothers went under, Credit Suisse hired him to run their retail group. After a couple of years, his family wanted to move back to the United States. He still had a house in Connecticut. I saw him in London, and I had a hole at Financo because Bill Susman, our onetime president, had left the firm—and I asked Colin if he'd like to join. It was always difficult for me to hire bankers from the larger firms unless there was a specific reason they were leaving. The compensation and a potential bonus weren't the issue, but the options that bankers received could run into the millions and when they were coming from a larger firm, we could not afford to transfer them to Financo. But we worked things out, and Colin moved back to the United States and joined Financo, and he was a real benefit to us, especially in London where our business was thriving.

But in New York there was stagnation afoot. What Financo required was an infusion of capital to keep the firm alive and growing. I was at an age where I was beginning to think about what Financo would look like after I was no longer there. Being in this position, although healthy but now getting older, I was unwilling to put in any additional capital. But beyond new capital, if Financo were going to continue on into the future—which was my hope—I would have to put a real succession plan in place.

Now, in general, the perception in the business world was that Financo *was* Gilbert Harrison. This had never been my ambition. In fact, when Steve Klein and I first started out, we had purposely decided to go with the name Financo as opposed to Harrison & Klein so as to create a firm that would be bigger than its two founders. But what would the perception of Financo be with me gone? What was its value? Would it survive without me? These questions were on my mind, naturally. Nevertheless, I had to put these large ideas aside and get to work on Financo's future.

To start with, Colin and I decided that the best thing to do would be to find a third person to invest in Financo and be an active part of the firm rather than just an investor. I had been in this position once before during the downturn of the early-2000s following 9/11 and took a similar course, and that had turned a great result. Back then, I had rekindled a relationship with Peter Ackerman, who I had originally met while spending time in Michael Milken's LA office. Now it was Marc Kaplan, one of the most famous lawyers at Skadden Arps, putting me back in touch with Ackerman, who was now an investor and founder/owner of Fresh Direct. Ackerman and I discussed the needs of Financo, and he ended up investing into the firm. It was an interesting arrangement—one that worked out well for us. Never designed to last forever, after a few years of renewed growth, I bought Peter out, and I'm glad to say we remained friends in the years to come. The experience taught me something valuable about bringing in new capital and a new figure at the firm with strong business leadership skills and a talent for growing. Mostly, it taught me that it could be done and done well.

And now I would have to do the same such thing again.

Colin and I went looking for a third party. We thought of other investment bankers that not only had good reputations but also capital. Indeed, we needed someone who could put in money and *a lot* of it. Many of those who came to mind had great reputations and, while earning plenty through base salaries and bonuses, still would not be able to put together the kind of initial investment we required. But by chance, we were talking to John Berg, who was a partner of a buyout firm in California and had also been Colin's first boss as well as someone I knew from doing business throughout the years. He had previously been a retail banker at Montgomery Securities and then at Bank of America, and he fit the bill. Turned out, his family wanted to move from San Francisco back to New York, and he had no interest in opening a one-man PE firm in the East. We had several conversations with John. He came to New York, and we had meetings with him. He flew down to Palm Beach at one point, and we had dinner where I introduced him to Shelley. We started to negotiate a deal. It was not the easiest deal. It took three or four months to complete. I used my lawyer in Philadelphia to do the agreement, which might have been a mistake. There were many loopholes in the agreement, as I found out later. After several months of discussions, however, we struck a deal for him to buy a portion of my shares of Financo and to put the needed money into the firm. And so, we were off and running. Again.

When John first arrived, it was very pleasant. We started trying to figure out how to move the business forward. John was very smart. He was professional. But then I quickly noticed some problems. In particular, I learned that he was very hard to communicate with. He would disappear. With other presidents and partners that I had, if I had questions, I could always talk to them in the evening whether it was Jeff, Bill, Steve Klein in the early years, Arnold, Colin...I could get them on the phone at any hour, more or less, so that we could talk through our business dealings. Open lines of communication are central to any business, especially as it concerns the people at the top. But with John, right away, there was a wall, and as the weeks and months passed, that wall built up higher and higher and higher.

As part of the deal, I had made John the CEO while I retained the title of Chairman. I would soon find out that bringing someone in and immediately making them CEO was a crucial mistake. A period of adjustment must be implemented. It became obvious once I made John CEO that things were going to be substantially changed. Some of those changes were good, but others were detrimental to the business. Perhaps if there had been some time before I made John CEO, he could have learned why certain practices were in place and had been for a long time at Financo, what their benefits were and what the cost would be of removing them. Instead, in my mind, the company suffered. For instance, he didn't realize—or perhaps he didn't care—that the way I had built Financo was to do a lot of smaller deals to generate fees in the $100,000–$250,000 range.

My good friend and early Financo President, Arnold Hoffman, puts its best in describing the foundations of our practices and philosophy:

> "When you look back, a lot of our business came from our contacts in Philadelphia and New York. A lot of the people we worked with were running family businesses, and they were uncomfortable with the Goldman Sachs and all the big guys, who would take their business, dump it into somebody's box, and it wouldn't go very far. And when they dumped it into our box, we took on the job and got it done."

Though these less prestigious deals might have not seemed important to a person like John who was only compelled to swing for the fences, the smaller fees they generated added up to a big number that paid the rent, the base salaries, and the overhead. Most importantly, those fees freed us up to work on the larger deals. The bonus pool came from the larger deals, which made sense since they were much harder to do and took a lot of time and effort. But now we were seeing fewer of these deals get done, the bonus pool was suffering, and several of our long-term bankers left because of this or were fired by John since I had yielded this power to him—and that hurt me deeply, as some of these people were like family.

Perhaps the moment that I recognized that I had a serious problem with John, though, was when I allowed him to get involved in the Jos. A. Bank deal. When the deal was done, we got a substantial fee, and he insisted that he get much more than he should have gotten. Where the bulk of the fee should have been part of my bonus, because he was chief executive, he wanted the larger sum. Remember, I had known Bob Wildrick for years. This deal didn't just fall in Financo's lap. In a sense, I had been working on it since the day I'd met Bob. But John didn't care, and it was very difficult, and I finally gave in. Though just one of several instances in which John asserted his control to ensure he was the highest compensated individual at the firm, it was in fact at this point in which I knew that John wasn't going to be a good partner and that he was all in it for himself.

So, there was tension. A lot of it, in fact. Then two things happened that changed our course again: first, Colin decided to leave because he found the working conditions difficult in view of the changes which had been brought to Financo. He received a phenomenal offer from a leading PE firm and chose to accept the offer, for himself, for his family, and his future professional development. Who could blame him? The circumstances were becoming untenable. And then John used his power from our agreement to move me from the corner office to a much smaller office. That's right: he took that unimaginable, sinful step and moved me from my office, taking the larger quarters for himself. That hurt me very much. It also upset those people who had worked for years at Financo. They didn't want to see me brought low. It was bad for morale, bad for business, bad for *everything*.

John had a different vision than I did, and he was trying to change Financo from Gilbert Harrison's company to *his* company. You could call me a serial entrepreneur. John was not that. He was more of a professional banker. He wanted to sell the company. Which, he eventually would do. And he wanted to get me out of the company, which he had begun to do since the moment he had arrived.

And look, I understand how it can be hard for a very aggressive president to find his voice and space at Financo. You have one president who was still in the industry, and he wanted to have that top voice and couldn't find it. And so, there was a lot of talking behind my back at Financo. I knew when the retail CEOs were deciding who to do business with, they were choosing other investment banking firms because there was so much infighting at Financo. There wasn't an aligned vision and strategy; we were coming at it from two different places. We weren't all on the same team, and that spelled trouble for everyone.

I knew that in order for Financo to move on, I had to retire and leave the firm I founded. Also, I didn't want to run fifty people anymore. And, it was succession. You have to chart a path forward and then stand aside for things to take its course. I wanted Financo to continue, but I wasn't willing to put in another three, five, or ten million dollars to keep it where it should be. Also, by retiring from that business, I could now go on and do many other things.

One night, around the time when it became obvious that I would be leaving the firm, Shelley and I were watching the film *Queen Victoria*, and when the queen died, her son became the king, and the final line in the movie was: "The Queen is dead. Long live the King." Boy did I ever relate to *that* line. Yes, if there was any lesson learned from that situation it was to realize that when a founder leaves and a new person is installed, the last monarch is dead, and long live the *new* king.

Probably the most upsetting thing I experienced in leaving Financo, though, was to lose the friendships and loyalty I had cherished with so many of the bankers at Financo. Obviously, John didn't want them dealing with me. That was an unkind lesson, painful. John was doing his best to turn my employees against me, knowing that I was going to retire. Perhaps of them all, the most hurtful act of disloyalty was with our General Counsel who had been with me since our days at Lehman. It became obvious that John wanted to fire this person on a number of occasions. I did everything I could to keep him secure at work and to keep him *in* his job—and then he turned on me. This is probably normal in a lot of corporate situations. But to have it happen to me presented a very unsettling situation. I totally trusted this person, and the actions that he took were unforgivable.

I recognize that I, too, might not have been the easiest person to work with. I had my failings. I had my actions. Sometimes I was too aggressive. But that's what made me. Would I have been more successful had I taken a different approach? Who knows.

The deal John and I had initially made was for a five-year transition period, and I would retire thereafter. But it was obvious that he had no interest in me remaining in the firm as the former Chairman when this time was up. I was unhappy and he was unhappy, and everyone knew it. It was time to take the next step. In our initial agreement we had determined how a buyout would work, and after some months of negotiating, we made a deal. There was tremendous tension at this time—for me, for Financo, and I imagine for John as well. Though I can't discuss my compensation, I can tell you that none of what resulted could have been accomplished without the help of Jack Nusbaum and his colleagues at Willkie to whom I remain most grateful.

Letting go of the firm I spent the majority of my life building was a difficult thing for me, but I felt it was the right thing to do so that it would continue on after I left. As you know, during my career, I advised so many clients that it would be to their advantage to sell their businesses. At times, we had the wives of clients crying at the closing like she was losing her baby. And sometimes, we had the founders themselves in similar states of emotional upheaval. In my case, stepping away from Financo was sad, of course. But I had thought long and hard about it, and with the advice I got from both Jack and Shelley, we went forward.

And honestly, there weren't many options. I had not been able to put a real successor in place. When my son, Edward, had come to work with me, I wanted him to be part of the firm and to takeover after I was gone. But I was perhaps too overly critical and not positive enough in my support of him, and certainly that was a shortcoming. It didn't work out with Edward, and I regret my role in that. When it comes to a parent and child and succession, it either works out tremendously, or it doesn't.

I was once with one of the great retailers of our time (I'll omit his name for the sake of this story), and we were talking about our families. I asked him why his children weren't more active in his business, and he said that he had given each of them over a billion dollars, and it had taken away all of their incentive to work for him. Incentive is everything, of course. You don't want to snuff it out.

But I do know of instances where bringing in the children has worked out phenomenally, and I am happy and proud for those families.

As I said before, there are all sorts of reasons why people hire us, but one of the major factors is that a founder doesn't think his children are capable of running the business and bringing it to where it should be.

Most of my career, I dealt more with entrepreneurs than I did with professionally managed companies, and there comes a point when it's obvious that the entrepreneur doesn't have the ability to bring the business to the next stage. As a result, they either fail or sell the company or bring someone else into the company. Those are the options. You take them. You live with them. That's the story.

If I could think of a happy variation on this story, though, it would go back to Home Depot and Bernie Marcus, one of the great entrepreneurs. Bernie asked me to find him a buyer and *I did not.* Left in this position, Bernie then took the company, put it on his back and brought it up to its new heights. I think that is an extremely important lesson. There is always the possibility of discovering that next gear and flourishing. But that's so rare.

I had more or less known that John would immediately look to merge Financo into a bigger entity within a year after I was paid out. What is interesting is that in many deals we ask for what is called "schmuck insurance," which means that if, after a certain time after a deal is closed, the company is sold for more than you were paid, then, as the seller, you receive a portion of the profit. In my case, we considered this kind of insurance very seriously but felt it was more important to close the deal since Jack and I weren't sure we trusted John or whether he could raise the money to pay me off. At that point, my relationship with John had deteriorated so far, all we were interested in was getting paid and getting out. I still don't know where John got the money to pay for my shares, but we assumed he might have taken on obligations afterwards that would force him to sell the company.

Usually, the "schmuck insurance" clause has an expiration date of twelve months after the closing and payment is made. In this case, I understand that John hired an investment banking firm to sell the business and eighteen months later (even with the lost momentum from the pandemic) Financo did announce a deal to sell. The buyer was Raymond James, and news of the deal broke in December 2020. It was upsetting, but I was not totally surprised. Remember, in many ways Financo was Gilbert Harrison, and I guess John did not want to take the chance that it would not survive.

To show the difficulties of a founder leaving a firm and bringing in a successor and the uncertainty of the results, that, more than the sadness of these events, is why I share this story here.

After I left Financo and was not asked to stay in any capacity, I moved my office to 745 Fifth Avenue and took two offices—one for me, facing Bergdorf's and Central Park, and one for my longtime assistant, Amylou—and the Harrison Group was born. A number of my friends worked in the same building or on the floor, and while it was not the same as what I had before, it agreed with me. The location was great, just a block from my old office. My club, the Harmonie, was just two blocks away, as were many of my usual lunch spots. But the thing I missed most was the interaction with my colleagues. It is interesting that during COVID, this problem has struck all of us deeply. I think about my own grandchildren, unable to go to school and having to learn remotely. What will happen in the long term is difficult to predict as we are coming out of the pandemic now, and many firms are allowing their employees to continue to work remotely. However, being able to use video conferencing platforms has been very beneficial, and no question it will continue to be going forward. I have clients throughout the United States as well as many foreign countries, including Mexico, the UK and elsewhere, and would typically have to travel to meet with them maybe once a month for a two-hour meeting. This would ordinarily result in a two-day trip. Instead, we were able to accomplish a lot through video calls, and while not exactly the same with dinners and visits, the savings on business travel, hotels, meals, and the time it takes to do all of the above, are nothing less than groundbreaking. My client eShopWorld (ESW), the leading global e-commerce logistics company, is based in Dublin. I am chairman of their retail advisory committee, and we now have weekly Zoom calls with our advisory panel. The people are in LA, Dublin, New York, Madrid, and Hong Kong and sometimes elsewhere in the world, but we're all brought together with the press of a button. This would have been impossible before Zoom took off. It's fantastic. Why would we want to go back to how things were beforehand?

Through my friendship with Bob Swindell at GLC Advisors, I became a Senior Advisor there. I remain there to this day, and we have worked on several deals—one of which I hope will be done prior to this book being published. It could be my "last hurrah" or perhaps even the "crown jewel" of my career, although at present, both the Marshalls/ TJMaxx deal and the Jos. A. Bank deal would fit that description.

I also became a Senior Advisor to Li and Fung, the leading sourcing company based in Hong Kong. I continue to be retained by Xcel Brands and others and have become more involved in public service with UJA and their Fashion Group where I was the Chairman along with other non-profits. I joined the board of my long-term client InterParfums, the global fragrance company headed by Jean Madar and Philippe Benacin. Shelley and I get to travel to Paris twice a year for their board meetings and also to Venice once a year for meetings for the Peggy Guggenheim Museum. And, more recently, I have been engaged by the Los Angeles-based company, Alo Yoga, to work with them on their global expansion, which is something I am greatly enjoying.

Gilbert with Jeff Bezos and Sean Combs at the Financo CEO Dinner in 2006.

CHAPTER 8

Land Ho!:
The Rise of E-commerce

WHEN THE INTERNET AND THE dot-coms were in their infancy, many of us had real questions about where the online retail industry was heading and whether or not it was even viable. There was a lot of disagreement. Right at the start, for instance, some people thought online retail would come to be 50 or 60 percent of all retail sales, and some thought it would be much more and that retail stores would become extinct. (I should note that many of the people who said this kind of thing were plugging businesses.) I admit that I was skeptical of online retail at first, maybe because of my age or maybe because I just didn't see the change coming as clearly as I should have. That said, however, I still took a very early leap into online retail and have remained deeply involved ever since.

As you may recall me mentioning, I was on the board of Bluelight. com when Kmart started the online company back in 1999. It seemed like there was great potential there. Unfortunately, the business did not work out. The problem was that most people didn't have home computers at the time and couldn't access e-commerce sites. Furthermore, after a period of unbelievable growth with e-commerce companies raising capital and going public at eye-popping values, in 2001—as many of you no doubt recall—the dot-com bubble burst, many of these businesses went bust, and discussions of the retail market being taken over by e-commerce all but stopped.

After the dot-com bubble burst, however, I still kept a strong hand in e-commerce. As part of Peter Ackerman's investment in Financo, we put a significant amount of money through our fund into Fresh Direct—the e-commerce food business which was then in its early days but steadily growing. Before you saw it everywhere, Fresh Direct had a terrific website for customers to go online and buy fresh groceries. They had put tons of money into their computer-automated systems. They had also built a tremendous warehouse facility. They were trying to compete directly with not only the regular supermarkets but also Fairway, which at the time was a rival (and is now bankrupt), and that certainly opened my eyes to what the future could be. In fact, seeing the possibilities, I tried to get Walmart interested in buying Fresh Direct, and Walmart executives paid a visit to the Fresh Direct facility one day at four o'clock in the morning, which was the time their operation was in full swing so as to be able to get the trucks out on the road. Though that deal never came to anything, today, if you take a look at Walmart and what others have done in the same business, especially with the growth of Amazon, it's spectacular. I also introduced Peter Ackerman to the Loblaws people, who were the largest grocers in Canada but had no internet or e-commerce business. The idea was that they could set up a joint venture in Canada and invest in Fresh Direct. But this deal never happened, in large part because of the skepticism and fear that one business would overtake the other.

When Jeff Bezos talked at the Financo Conference in 2006, he had already achieved a $70 billion market capital. Their growth certainly led others to consider the potential of e-commerce, and the term multi-channel retailing entered the retail vocabulary. (Multi-channel retailing is about working separately to achieve success, where omni-channel is about working together to do the same.)

As the growth of e-commerce continued, I saw firsthand the way American Eagle Outfitters, on whose board I sat, adjusted to the new reality and slowly made e-commerce a larger part of their business. Today it represents 35 percent of their total sales.

"When I agreed to join American Eagle at the end of 1999," says Michael Rempell, Executive Vice President and COO of American Eagle Outfitters, "both the Executive Team and the Board of Directors were incredibly excited and focused on the potential of e-commerce. We all wanted to figure out 'how high was high' and grew the business from just over $100,000 in 1998 to almost $20 million in 2000. Importantly, even after the dot-com bubble burst, the company remained steadfast in its focus on being a leader in technology and e-commerce. In 2021, AEO expects to achieve very profitable e-commerce revenues of approximately $2 billion, and our focus on technology and innovation is one of the reasons that AEO is a leader in retail while so many others have struggled or disappeared."

Other companies were slow to grow or ignored this change or just didn't understand how to market themselves to the online consumer. Among them was JC Penney. At its height, their catalog business was doing about $3 billion. But they did not see how to convert to online, and now that figure has dropped to less than $1 billion.

Today, as you might imagine, when you're evaluating any company, you really have to ask whether they are truly invested in the potential of e-commerce as a major part of their business. If not, the future of the business would already be in doubt. E-commerce has created global opportunities for many retailers throughout the world, and so many companies have been able to expand their market reach. Sure, there's been international expansion with brick and mortars, with Bloomingdale's going into the Middle East and Galeries Lafayette opening in China. But probably the most significant increase has been the reach of cross-border shopping through the use of e-commerce, and it is going to continue as retailers expand globally and look to tap into growing consumer appetites in emerging economies, especially in China and the Middle East.

E-commerce provides a capital-efficient way to quickly enter new markets, often by partnering with local stores, and stores need to enter new markets quickly in order to establish their presence and convey their brand to new consumers, as well as to prevent or avoid losing potential market share to competitors who have entered earlier. This is one of the reasons why I became chairman of the advisory council of ESW, as their global reach has been a very important way of having consumers see products all over the world. And now, I am consulting for ALO Yoga, the lifestyle and fitness company, in their planned global expansion.

Of course, in 2020, the pandemic struck, and people were staying at home. And what happened next? Well, we all know this story too: people still needed products, they were discouraged from going to stores, and so they started shopping online. The e-commerce market grew and grew—in some cases 300 percent or more—and this extended to global e-commerce distribution companies such as ESW, whose global reach has been spectacular.

As I write this book, it is obvious to me that continued change is inevitable. How many retail stores will close or downsize? How will delivery continue to expand? And will most new companies continue to be *only* in e-commerce? These are some of the big questions on my mind. More has changed in the last ten years than in the last one hundred, and who knows where we'll be even two years from now.

However, in taking a look at the way e-commerce has disrupted the market, there is, in my opinion, no way that the brick-and-mortar retailers and the malls themselves will go out of business. Yes, mall traffic is decreasing as people shift toward digital shopping. Yes, stores are going for smaller size boxes or even closing stores. And yes, the growth of Amazon and Alibaba and their increase in market share has certainly affected brick-and-mortar retailing. But people still love to shop, people still love to touch and feel the products, and so the brick and mortar will always remain a core of the business model. That's right, the brick and mortar is not simply going to disappear, and it's important that people understand that. "Bricks and clicks" will be the basis for all retailers continued growth.

As I finish this book in July 2021, it has been a most interesting career of which I am very proud. With respect to the investment banking, consulting, and financial services business that I have been involved in for the past fifty years, the changes have been enormous, and they are ongoing. In the preceding pages, I have reflected on many aspects of my career, but today it is exciting and interesting to try to understand what the future will bring. Certainly, with respect to merchandising companies, consolidations continue: department stores become less relevant, big-box retailer and specialty stores in malls grow but at a reduced rate, especially with the decline of foot-traffic. Most significant are the effects to both the retailer and the consumer as a result of the growth of the internet and e-commerce, both throughout the United States and globally. Now with the advent of digital currency, who knows where this will go. One thing that has been missing in the area is the introduction of new businesses. The big-box retailers, growth and decline of malls, the growth of e-commerce have all been tremendous, but in recent years, we have seen little in the way of totally new retail concepts with the exception of the rent-a-runway type companies and the pure e-commerce play. How will the landscape be changed? Again, it will be most interesting to watch and find out.

As for the greatest lessons I learned from over fifty years in business, first and foremost, one has to enjoy what one is doing in business. If one is not happy in their endeavors, there will be tremendous problems. I liked the people part of practicing law, but I did not enjoy the legal end, and this resulted in Financo, a people's business where I could use my legal background in mergers and acquisitions to excel in deals. I liked the ability to work with different people every day. Even as far back as my days at Precision Plastics, I knew I required variety. Who doesn't? It's just the essential ingredient. It always keeps it exciting.

Additionally, as mentioned before, when I sold to Lehman it was a new world, exciting. There is no question I learned a lot, but because of the politics and bureaucracy, I did not enjoy going to the office or attending to the work. The same was true of my last days at Financo. So, if there is any advice I can give you, it's this: make sure you enjoy your work, because you will most likely spend more time in your job then at home with your family or elsewhere.

And most importantly, never ever *ever* forget your family. They are still the most important part of your life, and many do forget this. In investment banking, there are a lot of divorces and affairs because of the constant pressure and long hours. In the end, we are all going to die, but hopefully those happy memories of your time together will remain with your family and friends. To be sure, those happy memories cannot live on through your bank account.

Gilbert with President Joseph R. Biden, Jr. in the 1980s.

| CHAPTER 9 |

A Few Words on My Relationship to the President of the United States, Joseph R. Biden Jr.

I HAVE HAD THE PRIVILEGE of meeting with a number of Presidents of the United States during my life, the first being John F. Kennedy when I was able to spend the day at the White House as earlier discussed. Also, I have met with Ronald Reagan and Bill Clinton. I was a member for many years at Trump International Golf Club in Palm Beach and spent a lot of time with the former President and I have previously discussed him with respect to licensing.

However, I have been especially privileged to know President Joseph R. Biden Jr. for over forty-eight years and was most excited when he became the forty-sixth President of the United States.

I first met President Biden right after he won his first election to the United States Senate in November of 1972. My brother, Roger, who is a longtime friend of his, volunteered for his 1972 Senate campaign after leaving his marketing position at General Mills. Starting in January 1973, Roger served as a top administrative aide in his DC office.

It was right after the election that my brother asked me to host a fundraiser for the Senator-elect in Philadelphia. The first of his fundraisers to be held outside of Delaware, I had about twenty people for lunch at the old Locust Club. Believe it or not, we charged the atrocious sum of $250 to attend. But it was absolutely an amazing time as the Senator-elect displayed those qualities and that grasp of contemporary issues that helped explain how a twenty-nine-year-old could win election to the United States Senate.

Our family followed President Biden throughout the years to come and saw the rise in his career. I visited him from time to time in Washington. I would see more of him in Philadelphia, where I held additional fundraisers, and did all I could to help him grow politically. It was a pleasure doing my part for President Biden—or Joe as I always called him.

I understood, and knew from the very beginning, that he wanted to be President of the United States. There is no question in my mind that this was his ambition.

I continue to hope that President Biden will be a uniting force. I know that he has always been able to reach across the aisle, and that he has been great at working out conciliatory agreements, and that he possesses all the skills needed to become a rival deal maker, should he choose to be one.

But as I write this book, it seems forces are in play that are making it even more difficult to continue his moderate stance, and he is being challenged in ways that test his ability to persuade others to embrace his vision. Parts of his ambitious and long overdue agenda are facing stiff opposition from the left and the right in ways that are pushing him away from many of his priorities. Finally, the fallback from our withdrawal in Afghanistan is something most disturbing and may change our perception of his presidency.

Regardless, I wish him the greatest success and will continue to advocate for him, always seeking to change the minds of those who question the value of President Biden's vital programs.

Gilbert with global CEOs at the Good Guys events held each year on the Friday before Thanksgiving. The occasion was seen as an opportunity for major retailers to get together for some joy before the start of the holiday season. Chaired by Marvin Traub, Burt Tansky, and Ira Neimark, Gilbert, because of his work with so many of the CEOs and his partnering with Marvin Traub, though a non-retailer, was allowed to be present.

| CHAPTER 10 |

The Proof Is in the Pudding:
Some Words from My Good Friends

<u>Mickey Drexler</u> (former CEO of the Gap and J.Crew)

"I love Gilbert because he doesn't stop—when he wants something, he keeps at it forever and ever. Which, of course, is one of the reasons he's as successful as he's been. He is not only a wonderful friend, but also one of the best dealmakers I have ever met."

**<u>Leonard Lauder</u> (Executive Chairman
and former CEO of Estee Lauder)**

"Gilbert has been the cornerstone in keeping the American cosmetic business on track. If it wasn't for him, we'd be all over the place, and that wouldn't be a good place to be! Thank you, Gilbert, for all you have done and continue to do. Most of all, thank you for being the great man you are and for the friendship you have shown me."

<u>Martha Stewart</u>

"He is so utterly debonair. He is so likable. He is so thoughtful. He is so generous, and he is always FUN. My type of guy!"

<u>Tommy Hilfiger</u> (Designer/Icon)

"Who doesn't LOVE GILBERT HARRISON! The ultimate dealmaker."

<u>Victor Barnett</u> (former Chairman of Burberry and former Chairman of Financo International)

"You have created and enjoyed over all the years a very successful and interesting business career, and you have made sure that you have been supporting the needs of institutions and those in need."

<u>Richard Baker</u> (Governor and CEO of Hudson Bay Corporation and Saks Fifth Avenue)

"You have been a mentor and a great supporter over the years."

<u>Bob Swindell</u> (Managing Director of GLC Advisors)

"After years of successful M&A and corporate finance transactions, Gilbert added restructuring expertise to his extensive skill set when he joined GLC Advisors as a Senior Advisor. His depth of relationships and knowledge of the retail industry have been invaluable to the overall growth of the franchise. With the rapid development of the omni-channel approach to consumers, we anticipate further consolidation and capital structure rationalization within the industry. Gilbert's expertise, experience, and relationships will continue to have a profound effect on the industry."

Sean Coxall (former President of Li and Fung)

"When I first met Gilbert back in 2019, he left an instant impression on me, a man of incredible drive, energy, with great listening skills and as sharp as a nail. I had taken over Business development at Li & Fung in the late Summer of 2019 and met Gilbert in New York City as he had previously been hired by Spencer Fung to help with business introductions as Gilbert has an impressive Rolodex of more than 6000 contacts in the fashion industry and has access to the C-suite in most large organizations.

During our first meeting over lunch in Barney's, I could see that we were going to get along. As we started to talk about opportunities, it was obvious how Gilbert could help me get in front of the key decision makers in a lot of the potential clients I was hoping to meet. We quickly made a target list and then got to work, and within a matter of hours I started to see e-mails flying back and forth and meetings already starting to be set up. As well as having amazing drive and work ethic, the one thing that stood out about Gilbert is that he did what he said he was going to do. Sounds very simple, but it's amazing how few people you meet follow this principle.

Within a couple of weeks, we started to have some really great meetings, doors started opening, and we started to sign new customers thanks to Gilbert's introductions. All was going well until COVID hit. I was actually with Gilbert in New York in February 2020 attending some of the key meetings he had set up, when I was called back to Hong Kong because of the pandemic. In September of 2020, I decided to leave Li & Fung after a twenty-year career to start my own company. At this time, Gilbert asked me to join the advisory board of ESW of which he was the Chairman. By November of 2020, we were up and running and started on a similar working path. This time, it was as much about the people I knew as well as Gilbert and how, together, we could help open the door for ESW to meet some of our joint contacts.

It's now been six months of me working on the ESW advisory board, and it's been one of the most enjoyable work experiences I have ever had. As Chairman, Gilbert ensures that we work as a team and help each other rather than competing, and he always comes up with great new ideas of how we can try to open a door or win an account. He always thinks out of the box and his comments are always on point.

I can only hope that when I am eighty years old, I have the same drive, passion, stamina, and energy level that Gilbert has, and also the drive to stay as fit and engaged in the world as he is. He truly is an icon, and I'm honored to have had the chance to work together with him in different capacities and learn so much from him."

Raymond Zimmerman (founder of Service Merchandise)

"I have known Gilbert and his family for over thirty-five years. We met at a Merrill Lynch conference, and I told him I wanted to buy HJ Wilson but couldn't. He said he could make it happen. And he did. When we talked fee, I agreed but told him he had a kicker after the deal closed, and the deal kicker was that he had to give $250,000 to the Jewish Federation and go to the international leadership meeting in South Africa. He stepped up and went. As I have told many people, if you want to Doral a deal, call Gil."

Kip Tindell (founder of The Container Store)

"They truly threw away the mold after him. There truly is no one else quite like Gilbert Harrison. He knows everybody. And he damn near knows everything, although, thank God, he doesn't act like it."

Robert Wildrick (former CEO of Jos. A. Bank)

"For twenty-plus years, Gilbert has been a confidant, friend, and advisor. He is honest, smart, and charismatic. But most importantly, he is loyal and extremely ethical."

Tommy Kelly (CEO of E-Shop World)

"When I sought to create an advisory group of retail industry heavyweights, I turned to Gilbert for guidance on the concept, and as the natural choice to select and engage the right people to join. Gilbert acts as the Chairman of the ESW Advisory Council, which supports our company's accelerating growth in the US and internationally in the beauty, luxury, and fashion categories. His in-depth industry knowledge and global reach enables ESW to engage at the highest levels with retailers and brands around the world to grow their e-commerce footprint and greatly enhance their digital sales capabilities.

Gilbert, as a person, is truly a joy to work with. He has an enormous, energetic personality that draws people in, and is truly infectious. This is reflected in his astonishingly massive and broad-reaching base of global contacts. Having worked with Gilbert for a number of years now, it is clear why he is one of the most respected, sought after individuals in the industry, and I am truly honored to have Gilbert as Chairman of the ESW Advisory Council."

<u>Stacy Berns</u> (founder of Berns Communication Group)

"Top 10 Things We Love About Gilbert:

- Gilbert Stops Traffic: Gilbert has stopped NYC traffic to make sure he was not late for his Bloomberg appearance.

- Gilbert Hosted the only "Must-Attend-But-Can't-[Get-]In" Party: Despite all of the networking events in retail, Gilbert created the only "must-attend" cocktail party/dinner in the industry.

- If Your Family Gets Sick, You Need to Call Gilbert: When you or a family member are sick, Gilbert is the only one to get you into any specialist that you need to see.

- If You Need a Wedding Dress, Gilbert Can Get You a Private Appointment with Vera Wang.

- Gilbert Has His Own Zoom-style: Gilbert is the only person who can conduct a Zoom video call while driving on the highway.

- Big Bark, No Bite: Gilbert has the largest bark but absolutely no bite at all.

- Gilbert Gives: Gilbert is the most generous and LOYAL person we have come across in business.

- Gilbert Knows Everyone: Gilbert knows everyone in retail and can get anyone on the phone, anytime, in any country.

- Gilbert Rides for Free: Gilbert is the only one who can get free entrance into the WWD CEO Summit, Shoptalk, and World Retail Congress, all expenses paid, with the best room in the house.

- Gilbert Put BCG on the PR map...and kept us here for almost twenty years and counting, but more importantly, he is our friend for life."

Bob D'Loren (founder and CEO of Xcel Brands)

"While serving at the helm of Financo, I admired Gilbert as a fierce competitor. In more recent years, I have come to know Gilbert as a brilliant advisor, confidant, and trusted friend. On Wall Street there are bulls and bears, but we often forget that there are lions too. The lions of Wall Street are the defenders of great intelligence, integrity, and wisdom. Gilbert is and will always be one of the immense lions of Wall Street investment banking."

Richard Braemer (my original attorney)

"While Gilbert was always determined to achieve a desired result, such determination did not detract from his unique charm."

Sir Ian Cheshire (famous UK businessman)

"I have always enjoyed your company and respect your take on the global retail world, but most of all, I have loved your sense of fun and the fact that it has always been the people you worked with that made it worthwhile."

Solomon Lew (Australian businessman)

"It was 1985, in Washington, DC, when we met and cemented our friendship at a special function for Israel philanthropy. I remember that night very well. We were sitting at the table with you and Shelley, and at that time, you were still living in Philadelphia. You were a major player in investment banking, and I recall how impressed I was with your knowledge of the retail import and manufacturing business, which I was also involved with at that time. Over the years, we have built a very solid friendship and managed to navigate our way through business and personal relationships.

In life, if you come across a dealmaker as good as Gilbert, you will do well. He's smart, well-connected, pushy, tenacious and relentless. When Gilbert walks into a forum anywhere in the world, he gets mobbed. Everyone respects him *and* his rolodex. He's a born dealmaker. He is one of a kind!"

Jean Madar (founder, Chairman, and CEO of Inter Parfums, Inc.)

"I have known and respected Gilbert Harrison for many years, and he was invited to join the Board of Directors of Inter Parfums, Inc. in 2018, where he is a valued member. Gilbert has been a relentless advocate for our fragrance company for over a decade, presenting us with suitable acquisition and licensing candidates, many of which came to fruition. As head of Financo, Gilbert represented Inter Parfums as we pursued a fragrance license agreement with the Oscar de la Renta brand in 2013. Then in 2014, he spearheaded our licensing agreement with Abercrombie & Fitch and its sister company Hollister. The following year, we made the largest acquisition in our company's history when we acquired Rochas, encompassing its fragrance and fashion business. Gilbert is more than a business associate; he is my trusted friend."

Sid Forbes (mall owner)

"Gilbert, you are one of the most knowledgeable people I know in the retail world. You have been a witness to the growth and all the changes that have taken place. It has been a great journey, and it will be interesting to see what the new norm will be. With your vision and knowledge, I am sure you will be involved on the leading edge of retail and its many changes."

Ari Pontz (Partner, Veritable, LP)

"At Veritable, we advise some of the most successful business people in the world. Gilbert represent[s] the epitome of that— entrepreneurial, hardworking, kind, intelligent, charismatic, with all the charms and qualities necessary to rise above the rest."

Dan Gillerman (Israel Ambassador to the UN and Financo advisor in Israel)

"During my tenure as Israel's Ambassador to the United Nations, Gilbert was always a wise councilor and has since became a business partner and a true friend."

Mike Gould (retired CEO of Bloomingdale's)

"We love Gilbert for his true friendship, his unbridled optimism, his energy, and his belly laugh."

Arnold Hoffman (former President of Financo)

"We all have to be a bit lucky to succeed in what we do and who we work with, and working with Gilbert was the ultimate experience."

Chris Blakeslee (President ALO Yoga and Bella Canvas)

"I began working with Gilbert upon his 80th birthday, and I remain impressed and envious of his sharp insights and drive, clearly from a career of being in the game. I hope I'm able to add value and remain as motivated when I'm at that point in life."

Karen Katz (former CEO of Neiman Marcus)

"Gilbert is the ultimate dealmaker. Whether a deal presents itself or, even better, when Gilbert invents the deal, there is NO one better."

Chuck Lubar (international lawyer and one of my oldest friends)

"I love Gilbert, but it certainly didn't start that way. I was ten years old and met Gilbert at Camp Robin Hood in New Hampshire. He was already notable in those days for his dark bushy eyebrows and his serious demeanor. The scene shifts to Nantucket, in the very late '70s, when my wife and I were trying out Nantucket as a summer destination. Just having landed from London, somewhat disheveled, and with me sporting a beard, we wandered the beach to see the annual sandcastle contest. We came upon a most beautiful sand carved mermaid with lovely blonde seaweed hair, behind which stood a very smiley and self-satisfied family. I looked up and spontaneously spouted: 'Your name is Gilbert Harrison, and I haven't seen you in twenty-five years.' Immediately, Gilbert retorted: 'And who the fuck are you?' That was the beginning of a long and continuing friendship.

Now I've known Gilbert for almost 70 years and our families have been good friends for at least 40. My wife Dominique and I have traveled together with Gilbert and Shelley to three continents and many exotic locations. I have seen Gilbert grow from his earliest days in building Financo to becoming a recognized titan in his deal making world. Through it all he is [a] great family man as husband, father and grandfather. Congratulations, Gilbert, on your accomplished life—and may it continue!"

Seth Lehr (an important Financo associate who really helped grow the firm)

"Gilbert could attend a business function with a hundred guests, and by the end of the night, he would have met the one person who had a business to sell and have a meeting booked the next day. Early on, Gilbert specialized in retailing and became a leader in banking the sector. He had an innate feel for the quick pace and entrepreneurial spirit of the industry and was befriended by both the senior statesmen of the time (Milton Petrie of Petrie Stores, Frank Rooney of US Shoe, and Stanley Goldstein of CVS, to name a few) and the up-and-comers (Les Wexner of the Limited, Don Fisher of the Gap, and Will Posluns of Dylex). Gilbert's approach to deal-making was old school. On the sell side, he would learn everything he could about his client and their business and then figure out who the best suitor would be. With that in hand, he would reach out to just a handful of parties and truly arrange a marriage versus canvassing the universe to arrange a shotgun wedding."

Norman Matthews (former President of Federated)

"Gilbert has the biggest business Rolodex of anyone. It's a wonder that he hasn't developed a cauliflower ear. He really is an astute financial mind."

Ian McGarrigle (Chairman of World Retail Congress)

"We love Gilbert because he has been such a fantastic sup-porter over many, many years; because he has always offered to help in any way he can; because he loves the retail industry and the people in it; because he has to be one of the most con-nected and respected people in the industry; because he is a good friend."

Marigay McKee (former head of Harrods and President of Saks)

"Twenty-five years and counting and he's been a great friend, adviser, and mentor to me."

Jack Nusbaum (my lawyer and a very good friend who passed in February 2021)

"Since our joint graduation from Penn in 1962, Gilbert has been a great and loyal friend and someone who could always be counted on to be there if needed."

Steve Sadove (former CEO of Saks)

"Gilbert has been a source of wisdom and relationships span-ning generations of retail leaders and has seen it all. He is smart, knowledgeable, connected, and always there with a word of support. I have valued his counsel for years."

Amylou Sarion (my trusted assistant of twenty-five years)

"I joined Gilbert in 1995 from the Leslie Fay Companies, a large apparel manufacturing company, which at that time was embroiled in a big accounting scandal. Gilbert was looking for an assistant and John Pomerantz and Alan Golub, Chairman and President respectively of Leslie [F]ay, referred me to Gilbert. I had already heard about him and spoke with him since he was pitching to help the company during this crisis. But Leslie Fay hired Alix Partners instead.

During my interview, he immediately insisted for me to take dictation and type up two letters. One was to Jay Schottenstein and the other to William Fung. I must have passed with flying colors—even if I was not released from Leslie Fay yet, Gilbert already wanted me to start. I did!

What Gilbert wants, he gets. Before ACT and Outlook, Gilbert had two massive metal rolodexes that I guarded with my life. To date, it became a standard for me to enter contact information of anyone we have met. Sometimes, Gilbert even forgets who he has in our contacts, some 13,617 names. To date, a phone number that I do not have to look up is Jay Schottenstein's number. I must have called him a million times, his number is imbedded in my brain.

I was so proud to be part of the TJX Marshalls deal in 1995. It was intense and I would work almost 10 hours-a-day and experience the excitement watching Gilbert and his team throughout the whole process of negotiations. The same is true of the time during the twilight of our Financo days, with the Jos A. Bank-Men's Wearhouse transaction.

Gilbert always wants things he needs *yesterday*. Before he learned to master the computer, he would dictate long letters and when I was transcribing, no one was allowed to talk to me. I couldn't even answer the phone until I had finished with what he had to dictate.

Gilbert finds it hard to accept no for an answer. If ever a client declined, Gilbert would very politely ask the reason why. I am not sure if a potential client ever changed his mind. But I do recall instances when a deal was dying, and Gilbert was able to breathe life into it.

Our small retirement party at Fred's at Barneys was thoughtful and nostalgic. At that time, I am not sure if I felt sad to say goodbye or relieved to be free.

One day, Gilbert gave me a piece of paper to file (I do not know where it came from). I wondered what was so important about this piece of paper, but his wish is my command. That piece of paper listed the qualities of leadership. Now I know why he had me file it! Through the 26 years I worked with Gilbert, I realized that he embodied all the qualities that were listed in that sheet! Gilbert has an immense passion for his work. He is very personable and exudes confidence. He is able to communicate with everyone. He has a clear vision of what he wants to do and is very focused on achieving his goals. Gilbert tries to excel in everything he does. He is aggressive and tenacious. He believes in his clients and where they are headed. Gilbert is able to adapt to this dynamic world. He has all the qualities of being a great leader and negotiator. That is why I stayed with him, not only for the money he pays me, but because of his respect and trust in me. And in the second phase of our business career, he has proven his valuable experience and business reputation to successfully start a new endeavor, the Harrison Group. I believe in him. His loyalty to his clients, friends and above all his family is most admirable."

Denise and Andrew Saul (clients and good friends)

"So many years. So many memories of shared dinners, business successes, art collecting, Nantucket, and most of all, family. It's difficult to know where the years have gone, but thankfully the memories remain."

Bill Smith (former President of Finance at Financo)

"He possesses great intellect and entrepreneurship which allowed him to build a great brand. He is loyal, sometimes to a fault. He believes in, expects strong performances, and respects all who partner and work with him."

Joe Stein (my stockbroker and friend)

"He is a friend we can always count on. His family always comes first. He is willing to reach out to all with his extensive Rolodex."

Steven Tishman (Global Head of M&A of Houlihan Lokey)

"He cares. He went out of his way to help my career. He is a loyal and supportive friend."

Bruce Toll (friend)

"Good friend, generous, gallant, gregarious, industrious, intelligent, loyal, loving, brilliant, economical, energetic, tenacious, take-charge—Gilbert."

Stuart Weitzman (Shoe Designer and founder of Stuart Weitzman)

"I shall start with Mr. Howard. That's when we first met. I still do not know how you convinced him to invest in me as all others seemed to be afraid of hopping onto a business that was a one-man show. But then that's why you are Gilbert. And as you know, it didn't end there. The second time around, you found the Jones Group. I'm not going to present that you were always right, but I will say you are relentless, so when Jones didn't work out, you became the catalyst that sparked our final sale to Coach. I think you're aware I'm not giving up on maybe trying for a fourth buyback and sale. It still bothers me that Lionel Levy is one up on me in that category.

As our friendship evolved, I became aware of the time and the support you gave to our alma mater, a great example to those around you about the importance of giving back. It certainly rubbed off on me as Penn now takes a good part of my free time. Well done.

You have always been my best source of what's happening in our retail and fashion world. It is not easy to engage one in such quiet conversation, so when I finally got to know you well, it certainly made for some interesting and appreciated dinner talk.

You have the most wonderful family. Of course, an equally wonderful wife helps make that happen. You and Shelley are proud of that, I am sure; maybe, Gilbert, your most rewarding achievement."

Gilbert with his entire family in the summer of 2020, gathered in celebration of his eightieth birthday and his fiftieth wedding anniversary with Shelley. From left to right: Henry Harrison, Joseph Harrison, Teddy Kaplan, Robin Kaplan, Jeffrey Kaplan, Caroline Kaplan, Susan Harrison, Ed Harrison, Shelley Harrison, Gilbert, Nancy Lascher, Jerry Lascher, Michael Lascher, and Harry Lascher.

ACKNOWLEDGMENTS

WHEN IT COMES TO ACKNOWLEDGING people in my life, I would be remiss if I did not start with my family.

First, my mother, Trese (Terri) Warner Harrison, inspired me with her confidence to be a successful businessman and of course my father, Daniel Lewis Harrison, who was always supportive.

While I have discussed my wife Shelley over these pages, I must again state how important her support has been for me throughout my life. We have now been married for over fifty-five years, and while not agreeing with all my choices, she has been a true and supportive partner while raising our three terrific children, Edward, Robin, and Nancy. She shares my adoration of our six grandchildren, of whom I am most proud. I could not have achieved what I did without, not only Shelly, but all of my children.

My oldest child, Ed, attended the University of Michigan, the College at the University of Pennsylvania, and got his MBA from Wharton. He has worked at Financo, McKinsey, Sears plc in London, a hedge fund, the Mercantile Capital Partners fund, and now is building his children's business, EGG New York. He is married to Susan Potok, a budding real estate star, and they have twin boys, Henry and Joseph, who we enjoy very much.

My daughter Robin attended the University of Pennsylvania and then Cardozo School of Law. Thereafter, she practiced at Schulte, Roth, and Zabel and married Jeffrey Kaplan who has a successful private equity real estate firm. Their children Teddy and Caroline are terrific. Teddy graduated from Wharton this past spring and has started working at Morgan Stanley. Caroline attends Wharton and runs a most successful business, Task Me.

Nancy, my youngest, endured our moving to New York to enter the big city. She graduated from Penn where she met her husband Michael Lascher, who is now a partner at Blackstone. Nancy then went to Columbia Business School and has worked at Ralph Lauren and American Express, and she is now a star at BeautyCounter.com. Their children, Jerry and Harry, make up the balance of all of my accomplished grandchildren. Jerry along with Caroline both have emerging entrepreneurial talents, and Harry is an accomplished chef.

All of the above-mentioned are my strongest cheering section, and for that I'm grateful.

I also want to say that my brother, Roger, is most important to me, as is Shelley's brother, Marshall.

I would be remiss if I did not acknowledge both of my assistants, Joan Casel, who started with me in 1974 as Financo began to grow and who assisted me through my move to New York, and of course, Amylou Sarion, who has now been with me for over twenty-five years and has stayed with me since relaunching Financo and today at Harrison Group. She wants to retire, but I am not sure how I could survive without her help.

My first boss was Milton Mermelstein, and I discussed working at his law firm in the book. He was a senior partner at a much larger firm and left to start Mermelstein, Burns and Lessor with two younger people from Sullivan & Cromwell. They taught me a lot during my three years with the firm.

I previously mentioned Sam Blank, who was the founder of Blank Rome. He was a truly wonderful person. He gave Steve and me a lot of advice when forming Financo. Sadly, he died from Alzheimer's at an early age.

From my initial days with Steve Klein to the present, there have been many people I have worked with that were special to me.

Certainly, Steve was a great partner for over thirteen years, and when we split up so that he could pursue real estate and I could continue Financo, there was no animosity. As for Arnold Hoffman, the story begins when Oxford Pendaflex was looking to sell their losing file cabinet business and wanted to hire us to do it. Since neither Steve nor I had any idea about metal bending, I asked Arnold, a friend at the time, to help us on a consulting basis since his family was in this business. He went into Oxford and identified the problem. Oxford took themselves off the market. However ,the story had two very good results: the first being that Oxford was so pleased that they paid us a bonus even though they had no obligation to do so; and, the second being that we asked Arnold to join us at Financo. He was terrific. Not only did I make him President when Steve left Financo, but he continued on after we sold to Lehman even after I left in 1989. We still speak all the time.

Other people at the first Financo meant a lot to me: Seth Lehr, who joined us while getting his MBA at Wharton, rose to be a most important asset of ours and continued with us until after we sold to Lehman and then started a highly successful private equity fund. We also hired another Wharton person to be our CFO, Sharon Lewellyn, and she was terrific and continued in that role even after we sold to Lehman. When I left Lehman, I asked her to move to New York to be both our CFO and COO, and she set up our entire office. She was with us for probably five years after I bought back the firm. But then one day she came to me to say that Steve Schwarzman had offered her a role to be a personal assistant to him at a salary almost three times what we were paying her. I was only proud that this had happened, and after leaving Lehman, she became the CFO of Evercore, which was one of the new boutiques, and helped take them public. A few years later she unfortunately developed terminal cancer, but I had her come into the office two days a week or so just to keep her busy. Sadly, Sharon died but at her funeral, the three eulogies were from me, Steve Schwarzman, and Roger Altman, who was the CEO of Evercore.

After Sharon's sad passing, Scott Abrams took over the role of CFO at Financo and helped me in working through my various finances. He has been the most loyal of all my ex-Financo people, and for that I am grateful.

Marc Leder was another person who joined Financo after graduating from Wharton. He was very smart and started in our Philadelphia office, but I also moved him to New York to work with me. He stayed at Lehman after I left, but a year or so later, he also departed Lehman and formed Sun Capital Partners with another Lehman person. He has been quite successful, and I have been one of his investors.

At Lehman, I also worked with many talented people, especially Peter Solomon, who I've discussed before. He and Sherman Lewis were the two co-Chairman of the Investment Banking Group which was where I reported to. Peter left Lehman about six months after I did to form his own firm that certainly was one of our biggest competitors. When I came in at Lehman in 1985, Dan Good also joined from EF Hutton to run the takeover business and buyout fund. He was someone else that I have remained close to, to this day. Peter Cohen, who was the CEO of Lehman, was someone I had to deal with, but his President Jeff Lane became a dear friend and remains one. Jeff also left Lehman and went on to be a Vice Chairman of Citibank and the CEO of Neuberger.

After leaving Lehman, because of working on deals together as I discussed before, we set up separate offices in the World Trade Center in what was Sandy Weil's office. I took my assistant and another young banker, Josh Goldberg, who was Peter Solomon's cousin and whose family owned Stop & Shop. Although Josh was very helpful to me for many years, his actions when leaving Financo is one of the most disappointing experiences I have had. So, there was initially just the three of us until we moved uptown. Then Sharon Lewellyn joined us and we also brought in Jeff Branman, who left First Boston to join us. We hired others along the way, including Karen Goodman, who was recommended to us by Les Wexner since she had done some work for his company while getting her MDA at Ohio State. She was in many ways my alter-ego and I miss working with her on a daily basis. When Jeff left, we brought on Bill Susman who had left Merrill Lynch as President, and he was with me for around seven years but left in an unpleasant situation. We then brought in as President Colin Welch, who I knew from his days at JP Morgan. Colin did an excellent job in rebuilding the firm, until, unfortunately, he left.

One of my early relationships during my days at Mermelstein and continuing through the years to follow was Lionel Levy of Shoe Town. Originally representing him as a lawyer and then as a banker, I sold him three times, and that most likely helped put my three children through college. Lionel had not one but two Rolls Royces, which was a feat in those days. He had a wonderful driver who was with him everywhere. It was interesting as when we sold his company to Fred Haddad in West Virginia, he said he could not have anybody working for him that had more than he did. So, he went out and bought a Rolls Royce but put it in his garage—on blocks no less—and only took it out to pick us up at the airport when we came to town. All jokes aside, Lionel taught us a lot about being a good retailer. Whenever we visited a store in a strip mall, he always parked far away from the front entrance because he said the customer comes first. As I traveled with other retailers, this allowed me to see who the winners were and who really loved their customers. Lionel and I became very close and continued to be throughout the years when we were both in Palm Beach.

Andrew Saul of Brooks Fashion and Cache, who just left as the Commissioner of the Social Security Administration, became a good friend. He called me his lucky charm. His wife and my wife became friends, and one of the most enduring things coming from our friendship was introducing us to contemporary abstract art, which Andrew and his wife collect passionately. Shelley and I retained their art advisor, and although our collection was nowhere near that of the Sauls, we love and are most proud of it. Coming from Philadelphia to New York before we moved here resulted in many dinners and much time spent together. They've introduced us to so many wonderful people over the years, many of whom we remain close with to this day.

In recent years when I started to do acquisitions for InterParfums, I became friendly with their CEO, Jean Madar, who lived in Paris. Not only did he invite me to join his board when I retired from Financo, but every year we travel to his home in St. Tropez for a wonderful time.

I mentioned before that I had met Sol Lew during the UJA International Council, and we also became close friends (though he lives far from New York in Melborne, Australia). Sol and I worked on a number of deals together although none of them came to fruition. However, our friendship resulted in our being his guests each year on his two hundred foot yacht in both the Mediterranean and the Caribbean for many fun times with he and his wife. We flew together to conferences, including ones in Morocco, Dubai, London and elsewhere, and he and I have always proven ourselves adept at mixing business with pleasure.

Tommy Hilfiger was someone I met when he was working for Murjani and doing the designs for Coca Cola clothes. Tommy and I would see one another throughout the years, and I inducted him into the Retail Hall of Fame during the World Retail Conference in Rome. Shelley and I love him and his wife Dee, and in fact, just had a wonderful time celebrating his seventieth birthday with them in Palm Beach.

Someone I talked to from time to time was Sam Walton, probably the most successful retailer in the world well before Jeff Bezos came along. Walmart was a growing company, and Sam was someone whose door was always open. If you called the Walmart switchboard or his private number, he would always answer the phone himself and just talk. Another person like that is Warren Buffet, and the several times I called him, he would also pick up the phone.

I had the opportunity to meet Dan Gillerman when he was the Israel Ambassador to the UN. We originally met when he talked at my home for the UJA Fashion Division reception. We became great friends, and when he retired from public service, he became our

Senior Advisor in Israel where we completed a number of licensing deals including Children's Place, Forever 21, Footlocker, and others. When we were in Israel, and when Dan and his wife were in New York, we enjoyed spending time together, and in Israel we met some of the highest government officials many times as a result of his graciousness.

I had the great pleasure of meeting Yasutada Oda through the Donna Karan people when he ran DKNY in Japan. We became fast friends and he introduced me to a number of the Japanese companies including Itochu. We later hosted their CEO at my home in New York.

Through my relationship with a number of potential clients over the years, I experienced some unbelievable adventures including having Fosun, which was one of the largest companies in China, host me at their Miss Universe pageant in Shanghai and also at the Global Forum there. I thank them for having me at these terrific events.

Additionally, we did work for Valentino. Among other things, we were retained by them to work on the acquisition of a large US retailer which unfortunately fell through because on the day the board was to sign the purchase agreement, Valentino received a buyout offer for the company. However, because of my relationship with them, Shelley and I were invited to the fortieth anniversary party for the founding of the company, which was held in Rome for three days. While we had attended so many events throughout our lives, this was probably the most extravagant affair we ever went to. It included a dinner in the Roman Forum and another dinner at the Borghese Gardens where they had built a pavilion to hold six hundred people at a sit-down dinner. My table companions were an Italian princess and Joan Collins. For these same festivities, there was also a fashion show and a Valentino retrospective in one of Rome's modern museums. Valentino, the company, achieved a lot of success from the party, especially since everyone attending had to have at least four different outfits, including those Shelley had to buy. A truly great event.

Another one of the most interesting parties we went to was the fortieth anniversary party for Ellen Tracy, which was held at the New York Public Library after the closing of the sale to Liz Claiborne. There were around two hundred people there for a sit-down dinner. We were at the back of the room and, frankly, I was disappointed, because I knew how much Herb Gallen liked me and that my work had made him a lot of money. The dinner was served and then the lights turned down, a curtain opened behind my table, and a stage appeared for Bette Midler. All of a sudden, we realized that the table we thought to be "in the back" actually put us in the front row for Bette Midler. A great lesson learned that evening, indeed: one should not take anything for granted.

As a result of Jeff Bezos speaking at our dinner, I had a running-dialogue with him and did suggest that maybe Amazon should buy FEDEX which at the time had a market value of around $6 billion while Amazon had a value of around $70 million and was losing money. I said that they could pay $12–$20 billion in stock and it would change the company and provide continuing distribution. Unfortunately, nothing happened.

But then, my Kindle broke and I thought to give Jeff a call—hey, why not?—and he graciously said that he would send me the new International Kindle which was coming out in three weeks. I said that this was most appreciated but that I would be traveling the next week and that I really wanted to take the regular kindle with me. So, what did he do? He sent me a regular Kindle to use on my trip and then three weeks later sent me the new International Kindle model. No wonder he is such a success, but, what a fool am I to have never bought any Amazon stock because each time I looked I thought it was too high. *Whooh.*

Isidoro Alvarez, who was the chairman of El Corte Ingles, was one of the great Merchant Princes in the world, and he did a phenomenal job growing his business, which is still the market leader in Spain. We did a number of transactions with them and also looked at the potential of them buying one of the major department stores in the United States before a recession came along. I will always remember the wonderful lunches I had in Madrid at his private dining room, along with Jorge Pont, who was the Chief of Staff for Isidoro Alvarez at Corte Ingles. Isidoro loved to come to New York especially during the Christmas season and shop in the department stores and see what was the newest and the greatest. He loved steaks, so I would take him to dinner at every great steak restaurant. When we went to the Four Seasons, of course he wanted to have steak there, and Henry Kissinger was at the next table over, which he loved. When we went to 21 Club, Tommy Hilfiger was at the next table over, and I introduced them, which resulted in Tommy Hilfiger clothes being sold in Isidoro's department stores. I was honored by both El Corte Ingles and the World Retail Congress to receive the first Lifetime Achievement Award in honor of Isidoro Alvarez at their annual conference in Copenhagen in 2015.

The person, however, that was extremely important to me was Jack Nusbaum. I first met him at Wharton in 1958, and he became the Chairman of the Willkie Farr law firm and a most famous and respected lawyer. He was one of my closest friends. He helped me throughout my business career, including representing many of my clients and advising me on my exit from Financo. He died this past winter and is really missed.

I would like to acknowledge the time that I spent at Camp Robin Hood, which has always remained a special place since it was there that I met my lifelong friends who have helped me in many ways including business, legal, and other opportunities. I started camp at Robin Hood at age eight and continued on for many years, and it was a major part of my early life. The groups—Tinker, Pager, Juggler, Squire—were all named after characters in the story of Robin Hood. When I arrived, in the summer of 1948, the camp had just burned to the ground in a forest fire and been totally rebuilt. I was so taken with the place, I remained there as a camper, waiter, counsellor and group leader, through the summer of my first year in law school. I have gone back for many visits in the past. Incidentally, my brother Roger tried to buy Robin Hood years ago, and today, the camp's co-owner is David Solomon, the CEO of Goldman Sachs. I went to camp with his father, so that important world keeps growing and growing. And that world continues to grow as this summer, my grandson, Henry, is a camper at Robin Hood.

I would like to thank Heather King, Debra Englander, and everyone at Post Hill Press for all their great work on this book. I would like to thank Jack Weiselberg for introducing me to JT, who was instrumental in the making of this book.

AUTHOR'S NOTE

IT HAS BEEN A PLEASURE working on my autobiography and a most enjoyable task to recount many of the things that have happened to me over the course of my life.

This book has been written for three purposes:

The first being for my family, so that they can know of my life and so that hopefully one day my great-grandchildren will understand what I have done and how much I have enjoyed both my family and my career.

The second is for my colleagues in the industry and the future deal junkies so that they can understand how my career has evolved and to share with them my experiences and the lessons that I have learned over the years.

The third and last is for my acquaintances and friends that I have dealt with over the years. From my early days in New Haven, to my present life in New York, Palm Beach, and Southampton, I appreciate everything you have done.

I am sure that there are many events, deals, and people that I have left out of the book. It is my hope that I have not offended anyone.

ABOUT THE AUTHOR

GILBERT HARRISON WAS BORN ON Christmas Day, 1940, in New York City. His family moved shortly thereafter to New Haven, Connecticut, where he was raised. He attended the Wharton School and then the School of Law, both at the University of Pennsylvania. His first job in law took him back to New York City where he practiced corporate and securities law. After moving to Philadelphia, he joined Blank Rome as an associate lawyer. Several years later, he and a fellow lawyer struck out on their own, founding Financo in the early 1970s. Their business rose steadily over time, becoming one of the largest boutique investment firms in the country. Financo was bought by Lehman Brothers in the mid-1980s, and Harrison began a difficult but intensive four-year period under Lehman—one that ended with his dissatisfaction with the banking firm and his eventual return to the helm of Financo. By the early 1990s, Financo, with Harrison at the controls, continued to be one of the true leaders in retail and other merchandising acquisitions. By 2020, after a long and successful run, Harrison sold his shares in Financo and started Harrison Group, providing financial services and consulting to its clients. The author resides on the Upper East Side of New York City, as well as in Southampton and Palm Beach, Florida, with his wife of more than fifty-five years. He has three children, six grandchildren, and remains busy as ever in business.